the Power of the Cross

Applying the Passion of Christ to Your Life

Michael Dubruiel

Our Sunday Visitor Publishing Division
Our Sunday Visitor, Inc.
Huntington, Indiana 46750

Nihil Obstat:
Reverend Michael Heintz
Censor Librorum

Imprimatur:
✠ Most Reverend John M. D'Arcy
Bishop of Fort Wayne–South Bend
June 29, 2004

Copyright © 2004 by Our Sunday Visitor Publishing Division,
Our Sunday Visitor, Inc. Published 2004.
09 08 07 06 05 04   1 2 3 4 5 6

Our Sunday Visitor Publishing Division
Our Sunday Visitor, Inc.
200 Noll Plaza
Huntington, IN 46750

ISBN: 1-59276-100-3 (Inventory No. T152)
LCCN: 2004111067

Cover design by Peggy Gerardot
Interior design by Sherri L. Hoffman
Interior art by Andy Kurzen

PRINTED IN THE UNITED STATES OF AMERICA

*For the word of the cross is folly
to those who are perishing,
but to us who are being saved
it is the power of God.*

1 CORINTHIANS 1:18

Behold, my servant shall prosper, he shall be exalted and lifted up, and shall be very high. As many were astonished at him — his appearance was so marred, beyond human semblance, and his form beyond that of the sons of men —so shall he startle many nations; kings shall shut their mouths because of him; for that which has not been told them they shall see, and that which they have not heard they shall understand. Who has believed what we have heard? And to whom has the arm of the LORD been revealed? For he grew up before him like a young plant, and like a root out of dry ground; he had no form or comeliness that we should look at him, and no beauty that we should desire him. He was despised and rejected by men; a man of sorrows, and acquainted with grief; and as one from whom men hide their faces he was despised, and we esteemed him not.

Surely he has borne our griefs and carried our sorrows; yet we esteemed him stricken, smitten by God, and afflicted. But he was wounded for our transgressions, he was bruised for our iniquities; upon him was the chastisement that made us whole, and with his stripes we are healed. All we like sheep have gone astray; we have turned every one to his own way; and the LORD has laid on him the iniquity of us all. He was oppressed, and he was afflicted, yet he opened not his mouth; like a lamb that is led to the slaughter, and like a sheep that before its shearers is dumb, so he opened not his mouth. By oppression and judgment he was taken away; and as for his generation, who considered that he was cut off out of the land of the living, stricken for the transgression of my people? And they made his grave with the wicked and with a rich man in his death, although he had done no violence, and there was no deceit in his mouth. Yet it was the will of the LORD to bruise him; he has put him to grief; when he makes himself an offering for sin, he shall see his offspring, he shall prolong his days; the will of the Lord shall prosper in his hand; he shall see the fruit of the travail of his soul and be satisfied; by his knowledge shall the righteous one, my servant, make many to be accounted righteous; and he shall bear their iniquities. Therefore I will divide him a portion with the great, and he shall divide the spoil with the strong; because he poured out his soul to death, and was numbered with the transgressors; yet he bore the sin of many, and made intercession for the transgressors.

ISAIAH 52:13–53:12

Contents

Introduction

I was going home in the spring of 1980 after a three-year stint in the United States Army, making my way along the rural back roads of North Florida. Just south of Cross City, I came upon a billboard that seemed totally out of place deep in the Bible Belt, where Catholics made up less than two percent of the local population. On the large billboard was an image of the Blessed Virgin Mary holding out a rosary. Underneath were the words, "Pray for the Conversion of Russia."

Later that week I mentioned the billboard to Father Pat Foley, the pastor of our small Catholic parish. He laughed. "Oh, Pearl had that put up, and it's created quite a stir." When I asked to meet Pearl, he suggested that I take the Eucharist to her at a local nursing home.

The halls of the nursing home were filled with old souls, some crying out in pain. I expected Pearl to be one of them, but when I arrived at her door, I found a young woman in her twenties. She was propped up in bed holding a crucifix in her arms, with a candle burning on her bedside table. Pearl smiled and invited me in. My new friend received the Eucharist with great devotion, then closed her eyes and made her thanksgiving while I stood nearby. She was an image right off a holy card.

For the next five months I continued to visit Pearl, until I left to attend college in southern Indiana. Several times each week I brought Pearl Holy Communion, then we would talk. Pearl had grown up in Michigan and moved to Florida after high school. She had been wild in her late teens and early twenties, she said, until life dealt her an unfortunate blow—terminal cancer. Now she lay abandoned in a nursing home; her husband rarely visited her, her family was far away. Although she had every earthly reason to be, she was neither sad nor dejected. In fact, she was the most joyful person I had ever known. What was her secret?

Pearl held up the crucifix she always cradled near her. "It's the power of the cross," she replied. Her sickness had helped her to rediscover the faith of her childhood; she had experienced the power of uniting her own suffering with the Passion and death of the Lord. She had relinquished her own plans and opened herself up to God's plan for her, even if it meant a short life on earth.

This book is the fruit of those meetings I had with Pearl almost twenty-five years ago. By her example, she taught me how to live in the power of the cross. That power enabled her to reach out and encourage others—the billboard was only one example of that. Pearl reminded me that, even when we are young, life almost never goes the way we expect. However, when we recognize the cross of Christ in those unexpected moments, we begin to find the answers to life's most pressing questions.

"Is This Really Necessary?"

Enter by the narrow gate; for the gate is wide and the way is easy, that leads to destruction, and those who enter by it are many. For the gate is narrow and the way is hard, that leads to life, and those who find it are few.

MATTHEW 7:13–14

Let's be honest: Most of us, given the choice, opt for the wide and comfortable path, the route of our own design. We would never choose the cancer, the unemployment, the infertility. The narrow way is just too hard, too lonely. Even so, the cross of Christ bids us to follow where it leads us. In John 21:18–19, Jesus prophesied this destiny for Peter, when he said: "Truly, truly, I say to you, when you were young, you girded yourself and walked where you would; but when you are old, you will stretch out your hands, and another will gird you and carry you where you do not wish to go." Sooner or later, as Peter discovered, a cross is offered to us. If we want to follow the Lord, we must not only accept it but embrace it.

At some point in our lives we must acknowledge that our ways are not God's way. We find one such example in the Gospel of Luke. On the day of his resurrection, Jesus encountered two disciples on the road to Emmaus. As they walked along they fell into discussion, and the two men shared with Jesus, whom they did not recognize, how they had hoped that Jesus was "God's Messiah" (Luke 24:21). Now these hopes had been dashed. Not only had the Lord failed to overtake his religious and political enemies; he had suffered an ignominious death at their hands. As far as they were concerned, God had abandoned Jesus.

At that moment, the disciples did not understand the way of the cross, did not realize that the road to victory was marked by overwhelming adversity, unthinkable suffering, and blind trust. All they could see was weakness, defeat, and failure; as a result, they were unable to recognize the Lord even when he was in their midst.

How does Jesus respond? "O foolish men, and slow of heart to believe all that the prophets had spoken! Was it not necessary that the Christ should suffer these things and enter into his glory?" (Luke 24:25,26).

"Why Didn't I See It?"

If you're like most people, there have been times in your life — if you're like me, lots of times — when you have said, "If I knew then what I know now, I never would have done that!" In reality, experience alone seldom gives us the wisdom we need to avoid all future missteps, whether days or years from now. As much as we like to think we know what is best for us and for those entrusted to our care, much of life is still beyond our control. It's frustrating — but it is also part of the human condition.

The Apostle Paul said it best in his letter to the Romans: "I do not understand my own actions. For I do not do what I want, but I do the very thing I hate" (Romans 7:15). It's called *concupiscence*, a fancy word for "disordered desire." As human persons, we do not always desire what is best for us. Not the way God does.

The good news is that it doesn't have to be that way. God became one of us in Jesus Christ to help us break this vicious cycle. He shed his blood to break the power of sin in our lives, and to restore us into relationship with God the Father.

Sounds great, doesn't it? There's just one small catch: We must be willing to be entirely transformed, starting from the inside. Everything must change: what we do, how we think, what we believe, and whom we follow. In the language of the Scriptures, we must "repent." This doesn't sound like great news at first — not to those who have deluded themselves into thinking that they are in control of their own lives. Yet to those who know better, it is the best news imaginable.

Still, it all boils down to the cross. Not the beautifully engraved golden ornament you can put around your neck and forget. It's the kind of cross Mel Gibson portrayed in *The Passion of the Christ:* full of pain and feelings of rejection, not to mention the blood and gore. The kind that requires you to die. It's frightening. It's agonizing. It's risky. It's nothing we would choose for ourselves, not in a million years.

Ah, yes. But it is also necessary. There are two things to keep in mind, to help you put this in perspective. First, once you understand the gift that is being offered, the risk is hardly worth mentioning. The way of the cross is the only way to eternal glory.

Second, the Lord does not expect us to walk this way alone. He gives us a helper, the Holy Spirit. He strengthens us through the sacraments, especially in the Eucharist where Jesus gives us his very life — body and blood, soul and divinity. My friend Pearl understood this, and received her Lord as often as she could. It was the incredible grace of this sacrament that gave her the strength to live out the mission God had given her to fulfill.

On the other hand, you don't have to be a spiritual "giant" to take up your cross like Pearl did. Those first disciples all fled when confronted with the cross of Christ at his arrest in the Garden of Gethsemane. They understood what was at stake, and they were afraid for their own lives.

Yet something happened between Good Friday and Pentecost. Something changed those men, so they no longer feared earthly power but trusted in Christ. Through the empowerment of the Holy Spirit, they sought to do the will of God even if it meant giving up their lives — and for most of them, that is exactly what it did mean.

Jesus extends the same invitation to you: Starting today, take up your cross. Forget the failings of the past. Don't worry about what tomorrow will bring. Open yourself to God's will for your life, with all its unsettling possibilities. Believe in the mercy of God that can withstand an honest appraisal of past sinful actions. Let go of your right to judge others or dictate terms. This is the power of the cross: In our weakness and humility, God's love reigns supreme.

"What Do I Do Now?"

Start reading this book. Each section is designed to be read and pondered on its own; read one of the entries each day, or take up one section each week. There are parts of this book with which you may readily agree; other sections will probably anger you. Don't worry about that; parts of this book elicit the same reaction in me. When faced with the cross, my inner demons rebel. Surrendering to the cross of Christ is the only way to get rid of whatever evil may be lurking in our lives.

The way of the cross is the only sure way to joy and freedom. The world offers us happiness and rejects the cross, to be sure, but it is a happiness that is short lived. For those who embrace his cross, Jesus promises a joy that never ends. The evil one makes it hard for us to see the truth of Jesus' claim at times. But those who seek the truth will experience — either first-hand or through living saints like Pearl — true reality: What the world promises is a lie.

We are all headed to Cross City, whether we are following Christ or not. For those who follow Christ, Cross City is the gate to eternal life. For those who venture along that path without Christ, the cross brings only suffering and ultimately death. The crucified Christ is the Vine; we are called to be the branches. May his joy be in you, "that your joy may be full" (John 15:11).

How to Use This Book

This book is not designed to be read in one sitting. There are seven sections or chapters, each containing individual reflections that can be read daily or through the course of a week. These reflections may be part of your private reading, or studied as a group exercise. If the book is used in a group, the material at the end of each chapter/day can be used as a guide for the group discussion and prayer. Additional questions for each chapter are found in Appendix I.

Each day's entry includes several Scripture quotes. The first reading relates to the topic being discussed. The second reading is always from the gospel of the day for Lent (from Cycle A on Sundays) with the first week beginning on the first Sunday of Lent. If you would like to use this book as a Lenten devotional please see Appendix II.

In the Gospel of Luke, Jesus says: "Ask and it will be given to you; seek, and you will find; knock, and it will be opened to you" (Luke 11:9). Each chapter of the book contains a section entitled "Ask, Seek, and Knock." This section, as well as the final "Transform Your Life" section, presents the reader with an opportunity to internalize the material: "Ask" yourself questions, "Seek" out the truth through action, and "Knock" by meditating on the Scripture so that the text may be opened to you. Finally, "Transform Your Life" challenges you, as the reader, to follow Jesus in a way you might not have considered in the past. Use what is helpful; pass over what is not.

"How Should I Meditate?"

Those unfamiliar with the Christian practice of meditation may benefit from this simple process. First, find a place without distractions, and make yourself comfortable. Then ask God to speak to you through his Word. Turn to the Scripture passage indicated (using a Bible or reading it from this book) and read it slowly, either silently or aloud. Allow the text to enter your mind and heart, pausing to reread several times parts that seem especially meaningful or personally relevant. Finally, pay attention to whatever God may be saying to you in these passages and bring that to prayer.

The goal of this book is to open you up to finding God's will by reflecting on your life and on God's purpose for you as seen through the light of the cross and the Scriptures. I would recommend that you say the following prayer every time you pick the book up as a way of opening yourself up to whatever God wants you to learn from this book as it applies to your own life. It is the prayer of St. Ignatius of Loyola:

Lord, all that I have and possess you have given me. I give all of it back to you, to use according to your will. Take my freedom, my past, my perceptions, my desires; give me your love and grace in exchange. With these I am truly rich and possess all that I need. Amen.

The Cross of Christ Teaches Us . . .

(WEEK ONE)

Resist the devil and he will flee from you. Draw near to God and he will draw near to you. JAMES 4:7–8

JESUS has always many who love His heavenly kingdom, but few who bear His cross. He has many who desire consolation, but few who care for trial. He finds many to share His table, but few to take part in His fasting. All desire to be happy with Him; few wish to suffer anything for Him. Many follow Him to the breaking of bread, but few to the drinking of the chalice of His passion. Many revere His miracles; few approach the shame of the cross. Many love Him as long as they encounter no hardship; many praise and bless Him as long as they receive some comfort from Him. But if Jesus hides Himself and leaves them for a while, they fall either into complaints or into deep dejection. Those, on the contrary, who love Him for His own sake and not for any comfort of their own, bless Him in all trial and anguish of heart as well as in the bliss of consolation. Even if He should never give them consolation, yet they would continue to praise Him and wish always to give Him thanks. What power there is in pure love for Jesus—love that is free from all self-interest and self-love!

Thomas à Kempis,
Imitation of Christ, Book II, Chapter XI.

Day 1

The Cross of Christ Teaches Us . . .
Our Mission

And the angel of the Lord said to him, "Why have you struck your ass these three times? Behold, I have come forth to withstand you, because your way is perverse before me; and the ass saw me, and turned aside before me these three times. If she had not turned aside from me, surely just now I would have slain you and let her live." Then Balaam said to the angel of the Lord, "I have sinned, for I did not know that thou didst stand in the road against me. Now therefore, if it is evil in thy sight, I will go back again." And the angel of the Lord said to Balaam, "Go with the men; but only the word which I bid you, that shall you speak."

NUMBERS 22:32–35

Then Jesus said to him, "Begone, Satan! for it is written, 'You shall worship the Lord your God and him only shall you serve.'" Then the devil left him, and behold, angels came and ministered to him.

MATTHEW 4:10–11

One of the strangest stories in the Old Testament recounts the mission of the prophet Balaam. A pagan king wanted to conquer the Israelites, and wanted Balaam to help him achieve this ambition by pronouncing a curse on the enemy. So he summoned Balaam.

At first Balaam refused to come, but eventually Balaam set out on his donkey to meet with the king. Although this story is found in the Book of Numbers, it is the Second Letter of Peter that gives us insight to Balaam's motives: "Forsaking the right way. . . they have followed the way of Balaam, the son of Be'or, who loved gain from wrongdoing, but was rebuked for his own transgression; a dumb ass spoke with human voice and restrained the prophet's madness" (2 Peter 2:15–16). Balaam was not setting out to do God's will; he was trying to profit by the gifts that God had given him.

Balaam was stopped en route by his donkey, which saw an angel barring the path. When Balaam beat his donkey, the animal protested that he was trying to save his master's life. Finally Balaam's eyes were opened to the angel of the Lord, who affirmed that, indeed, the donkey had saved his life. The angel told him to go along to the king: "Go. . . but only the word which I bid you, that shall you speak" (Numbers 22:35). In the end, Balaam blessed the Israelites, accomplishing God's purposes. However, Peter's epistle reveals that Balaam's temptation moved him along the path to do the will of God. He did not start out intending to do good, but God intervened.

Spiritual U-Turns

A friend once told me of the time he decided to give in to a certain temptation that he had been fighting for years. As he went to get into his car that night, he discovered that one of his car's tires was flat. Most people would see a flat tire as a momentary inconvenience; my friend saw the flat tire as a sign from God. He stayed home that night, and from that moment on the temptation left him. God used my friend's momentary lapse to put him on the pathway to holiness.

Scripture has many examples of God using Satan's ploys to accomplish his own purposes. The Gospel of Matthew offers one such example. When Jesus was about to begin his ministry in Israel, he went into the desert to fast for forty days—symbolic of the forty years the Israelites wandered in the desert. During that time, Satan presented three types of temptations to Our Lord. Ironically, each of the particular temptations Satan chose was related to the mission that God had given to Jesus. Each of them was a perversion of Jesus' true mission and purpose.

Bread of Life. First the evil one tempted Jesus to turn stones to bread. After all, Jesus was hungry from fasting. However, Jesus knew that his greatest hunger was not physical but relational: He had a hunger only God could satisfy.

The significance of this temptation became clearer on the night before Jesus died, when he took the bread and changed it into his own Body and Blood. "I am the bread of life," Jesus declared. "If any-

The things that tempt us most in life can lead us to discover our true calling.

one eats of this bread, he will live for ever; and the bread which I shall give for the life of the world is my flesh" (John 6:48, 51).

Those who partake in the Body and Blood of Christ under the appearance of bread and wine, wrote St. Cyril of Jerusalem, become "united in body and blood with Him." Similarly, St. Pio of Pietrelcina (Padre Pio) observed that after communion, "the heart of Jesus and my own—allow me to use the expression— were fused. No longer were two hearts beating but only one. My own heart had disappeared, as a drop of water is lost in the ocean." The miracle of the Eucharist is that Our Lord transforms our hearts of stone into hearts of flesh.

Source of Life. In the second temptation, Satan tempted Jesus to demonstrate his power by throwing himself off the Temple roof, so the angels would rush to his defense. Jesus recognized that his enemy had twisted Scripture to achieve his own purposes. "You shall not tempt the Lord your God," he replied firmly (Matthew 4:7).

As with the temptation to turn stones to bread, Satan's temptation was a perversion of the real mission of Christ. By dying on the cross, Jesus threw himself into the hands of the Father, trusting that God would raise him on the third day.

When Franz Jaegerstaetter, a saintly Austrian who refused to fight in the Nazi army, faced certain death because of his refusal to give in to the Nazis' wishes, Franz wondered if he were committing suicide. It was a meditation on the mission of Jesus, who went to Jerusalem knowing that they were going to kill him there, that finally convinced Franz that standing up to the evil of his day, no matter what the personal cost, was the right thing to do.

Prince of Life. Finally the Lord was tempted to bow down to Satan in order to win the world. However, just as Jesus rejected the attempts of his followers to make him king or to win the kingdom by the sword, so he rejected this bloodless solution.

Jesus knew that real victory would not come easily, and that his kingdom was not an earthly one. His message was not a popular one; ultimately it led to his death on the cross. This "King of the Jews," as the Romans named him, knew of but one way to win over the world: "...when I am lifted up from the earth, [I] will draw all men to myself" (John 12:32).

Those who would be powerful continue to bow to Satan in order to win the world, selling their souls for a temporary advantage. Politicians, religious, and others who promote evil in order to win—whether the prize is power, approval, or other earthly glory—may succeed for a time. But such victory is fleeting, and leaves in its wake an emptiness that is as close to hell as one can experience on this earth.

Find Your Mission

Just as Satan tempted Christ with a perversion of his true mission, the things that tempt us most in life can lead us to discover our true calling. However, we will recognize God's purpose for us only by the light of the cross. Using God's gifts to achieve anything other than the divine plan will not bring long-term satisfaction. The path to true joy comes from placing our gifts under the control of the Holy Spirit, and allowing the cross of Christ to reveal Satan's lies and deceptions for what they are.

St. Augustine, who spent his early years tempted by the beauty of creation and even fathering an illegitimate child, later found in God the beauty he was seeking. "Too late, O ancient Beauty, have I loved Thee," he wrote.

Steps to Take as You Follow Christ

Ask—What temptations do I find hardest to resist? How might this reveal God's intended purpose for me?

Seek—Reject sin. Learn to see in your temptations a perversion of God's plan for you. Try to discern what it is that God might be calling you to do by looking at the areas of your life where you are most tempted.

Knock—Meditate on Numbers 22:32–35. How does Balaam's ass differ from the prophet with respect to discerning the path God wanted them to take? Are you more like the donkey or the prophet?

Transform Your Life—Sometimes we live as though God does not see us, yet we know that God is always present, whether or not we acknowledge him. Look over your life and try to see where God has revealed himself at various moments in your life. Then move confidently into the future, assured of God's providential care for you.

Day 2

The Cross of Christ Teaches Us . . .
To Live the Gospel

For it is not hearers of the law who are righteous before God, but the doers of the law who will be justified. When Gentiles who have not the law do by nature what the law requires, they . . . show that what the law requires is written on their hearts, while their conscience also bears witness and their conflicting thoughts accuse or perhaps excuse them on that day when, according to my gospel, God judges the secrets of men by Christ Jesus.

ROMANS 2:13–16

Then the King will say to those at his right hand, "Come, O Blessed of my Father, inherit the kingdom prepared for you from the foundation of the world; for I was hungry and you gave me food, I was thirsty and you gave me drink, I was a stranger and you welcomed me, I was naked and you clothed me, I was sick and you visited me, I was in prison and you came to me."

MATTHEW 25:34–36

One day my mother came back from a day of shopping very upset. As she walked past a vagrant on her way into a store, the man had called out to her, "I'll bet you would take more time to notice a dog."

My mother was saddened and shamed by the man's accusation. In a way, he was right; she hadn't even acknowledged the man's existence. It was one short encounter in her busy life. Even so, I have never forgotten it, and neither has she.

In the Gospel of Matthew, Jesus spoke about the last judgment of the nations, and in particular the judgment of "nonbelievers," which is how the Jewish people referred to the Gentile nations. When, in his letter to the Romans, St. Paul indicated how those who do not know Christ will be judged, referring to the "gospel," very likely, he was referring to this passage from Matthew 25.

Those of us who know Christ have little excuse if we do not recognize him in the hungry, thirsty, stranger, naked, sick, or imprisoned. We have the good news of the gospel preached to us; we have heard it and are required to put it into practice.

Seeing the Hidden Christ

The people who experienced Jesus in the flesh, we know, all experienced him in exactly the ways that he describes in Matthew 25, and part of understanding that is a lesson for all of us. We do not know when Our Lord might appear to us under the guise of the hungry, thirsty, stranger, naked, sick, or prisoner.

I was hungry... Because he was fully human as well as fully God, Jesus had the same bodily needs we do. After fasting in the desert for forty days and nights, he was hungry. Several of the resurrection appearances have Jesus asking the disciples if they have anything to eat before they recognize who it is asking for relief from his hunger.

I was thirsty... "Give me a drink," Jesus said to the Samaritan woman at the well, just before telling her of the living water. From the cross he cried out "I thirst," and was given vinegar to drink.

I was a stranger. . . After his resurrection, Jesus was often not recognized, even by his own disciples. Mary Magdalene mistook him for a gardener. The disciples en route to Emmaus thought he was a stranger until he broke bread in their midst. The disciples fishing on the Sea of Galilee did not at first recognize the man on the shore, cooking fish and bread over a charcoal fire.

† *The Passion of Jesus reveals that God is present even when he seems farthest away. So we must not give in to the temptation to abandon those who seem to us crucified and rejected: the hungry and thirsty, the stranger or prisoner, the naked and sick.*

I was naked. . . At the beginning of his life, Christ came forth naked from his Virgin Mother, who wrapped him in swaddling clothes and laid him in a manger. At the end, his executioners stripped him naked before nailing him to the cross. His burial shroud, donated by Joseph of Arimathea, was left behind at the Resurrection.

I was sick. . . Suffering from the soldier's maltreatment, he burned with fever on the cross. Meanwhile, his enemies taunted him. "You healed so many others. . . now heal yourself!"

I was in prison. . . Imprisoned after his arrest in the Garden of Gethsemane, he went from the Sanhedrin, to Pilate to Herod and to Pilate again. At the hands of cruel Roman soldiers he was mocked and scourged.

How many times have we missed an encounter with Jesus? How often do we walk past the destitute residing on the street or in prisons, nursing homes, and hospitals, not realizing that we are passing by the Son of God?

"Be not hearers, but doers. . ." St. Paul told the Romans.

Do we act any differently when someone is watching us? We slow down on the road if we spot a police officer coming in the other direction. We work a little harder if our boss is nearby. Yet when isn't God in our presence?

The Passion of Jesus reveals that God is present even when he seems farthest away. We might even be tempted to think that God has abandoned those we choose to pass by. Yet nothing could be farther from the truth: "...as you did it to one of the least of these my brethren, you did it to me" (Matthew 25:40).

Almsgiving has always been a Christian penitential practice. It is one of the ways that we become more like Christ and take up our cross to follow him daily. Jesus gave to everyone who approached him; we, empowered by him, are called to share what he gives us with all whom we meet—and even those we must seek out.

Steps to Take as You Follow Christ

Ask—Where have I encountered Christ "in the least of my brethren"?

Seek—Make an effort to see Christ in the hungry, thirsty, stranger, naked, sick, or imprisoned. Try to reach out to those no one else notices.

Knock—Meditate on Romans 2:13–16. What are the secrets of your life that will be brought to judgment? How can you be more of a doer rather than just a listener of the Word of God?

Transform Your Life—Expect to meet Christ daily, first in the bread that is broken at Mass and then in the people who cross your path. See nothing as chance but everything as somehow fitting into the mysterious plan of God.

Day 3

The Cross of Christ Teaches Us . . .
How to Pray

In the days of his flesh, Jesus offered up prayers and supplications, with loud cries and tears to him who was able to save him from death, and he was heard for his godly fear.

HEBREWS 5:7

And in praying do not heap up empty phrases as the Gentiles do; for they think that they will be heard for their many words. Do not be like them, for your Father knows what you need before you ask him.

MATTHEW 6:7–8

While visiting the Holy Spirit Trappist monastery in Conyers, Georgia, I wandered into the abbey church one afternoon to spend a few moments in prayer. A young woman with two small children was already there. Although she prayed inaudibly as her two small children circled about her, I could tell by her raised hands and her tears that she was pleading and reasoning with God. I have no idea what the woman was praying about, only that she was praying the way Moses is described in the Letter to the Hebrews, ". . .seeing him who is invisible."

As the Israelites battled the Amalekites (see Exodus 17), Moses lifted his hands in prayer, holding his wooden staff over his head as the battle raged in the valley below. So long as Moses' hands remained in the air, the Israelites were victorious; as Moses' arms grew tired and began to fall to his sides, the battle turned to the enemy's advantage. When they realized what was happening, Aaron and Hur stood on either side of Moses, holding his hands aloft, until the battle was won.

To the early church fathers, the prayer of Moses with his arms outstretched foreshadowed the victory Christ won on the cross. Like Aaron and Hur, we have an opportunity to stand with Christ, interceding for the salvation of souls. Of course, Moses, Aaron, and Hur had an advantage that we do not: They could see the effects of Moses' intercession on the battle raging below. How our prayer life would change if God gave us the ability to see the effect our intercessions—or lack thereof—have on the battle that is being waged daily for souls.

The letter to the Hebrews draws a strong connection between the cross and prayer. Because every moment of our earthly existence is threatened by death, and we know neither the day nor the hour when that existence will come to an end, we, too, need to cry out to the God who can save us. Like Moses, we need the help of our fellow Christians to hold up our arms when they grow tired. We, too, need the help of the Holy Spirit to make up for what is lacking in our prayer.

Praying as a Follower of Christ

Throughout the centuries, Christians in the East and the West have signed themselves with the cross. When it is done with little thought or care, the sign loses much of its power. Contemplating both the action and what it symbolizes as you make the sign, on the other hand, is the perfect way to begin any conversation with God.

As you make the sign of the cross, you place your entire being in the shadow of the cross of Christ. By invoking the Trinity as you make this holy sign, you immediately call to mind that facing the cross is something we dare not do alone, but only in God's presence. Every moment, we must choose between the way of the cross of Christ and the way of perdition. Every minute, the battle for our salvation is being lost or won.

"Do not pray like the Gentiles," Jesus instructed his disciples. Some Christians see this as a prohibition of repetitive prayers, but clearly this isn't what Jesus was condemning. The admonition had scarcely fallen from his lips when he proceeded to teach his disciples one of the most beloved prayers of all time: the "Our Father," or "Lord's Prayer."

Not only did Jesus teach his disciples to pray using a certain form; in the gospels we read that Jesus himself prayed the same words over and over in the Garden of Gethsemane, "He went away and prayed for the third time, saying the same words," (Matthew 26:44). When we share in Christ's Passion we will often find ourselves able only to mouth the same words over and over.

The early disciples of Jesus, those most familiar with his teachings on prayer, developed litanies and other repetitive prayers. For example, the "Lord Have Mercy" litany has remained in the liturgies of the East and West to this day, and is drawn from several gospel accounts, most notably the two blind men in Jericho who voiced this prayer repeatedly in desperation to Jesus, and who voiced it all the louder when the crowd tried to rebuke them (see Matthew 20:29–31). Similarly, the Jesus Prayer ("Lord Jesus, Son of God, have mercy on me, a sinner") is taken from the story of a blind man in Luke's Gospel (see Luke 18:38).

In the early church, Christians prayed with their bodies as well as their minds. Congregants often prayed with their arms outstretched in the *"orans"* position, identifying with the crucified Christ as they prayed to the Father. There have been attempts to restore this practice within the church; others choose to pray this way in private. In this way not only do we imitate the cross of Christ, we acknowledge that all of our prayer is through Christ and in Christ. It is also a good way to express one's abandonment to God's will. As our arms tire, we remember that our strength cannot save us; we need help both from God above and from our neighbors below.

So what are the "empty phrases" of the Gentiles that Jesus condemned? He objected to the mindless offering of prayers without faith. While times of "spiritual dryness" are a normal part of the Christian experience, we must guard against "going through the motions" for the benefit of others, and persevere with faith and trust. In times of doubt, we must strive to embrace the cross of Christ in our lives. Refuse to give in to the passions, or to be held captive by sin. The way of the cross is the way of healing.

> The only thing that Jesus promised his disciples in this life was persecution. Many times we forget that; we get so caught up with the "cares of this world" that we forget about the cross that we are supposed to be carrying as followers of Christ.

As Father Benedict Groeschel rightly points out, the only thing that Jesus promised his disciples in this life was persecution. Yet many of us get caught up with the "cares of this world" and forget about the cross we are to carry as followers of Christ. May the cross with which we sign ourselves, and the cross we place before our eyes, always keep us mindful of what we are doing and what is at stake.

Steps to Take as You Follow Christ

Ask—How can my prayer better reflect what is going on in my life at the present moment?

Seek—Try praying for an extended period of time in the *orans* position. Ask Our Lord to teach you this lesson from the cross, so that your prayer might always be heartfelt.

Knock—Meditate on Hebrews 5:7. How might your prayer become more like the prayer of Christ?

Transform Your Life—Foster a sense of God's presence before you begin any prayer. Speak to God from your heart, then listen. God is the most important being with whom you will ever speak.

Day 4

The Cross of Christ Teaches Us . . .
About Repentance

For Jews demand signs and Greeks seek wisdom, but we preach Christ crucified, a stumbling block to Jews and folly to Gentiles, but to those who are called, both Jews and Greeks, Christ the power of God and the wisdom of God.

1 CORINTHIANS 1:22–24

This generation is an evil generation; it seeks a sign, but no sign shall be given to it except the sign of Jonah.

LUKE 11:29

Some years ago I visited the Florida State Prison, accompanying a group of men from around the state who converged on the prison one Saturday of every month to have fellowship with men convicted of the vilest crimes imaginable. I introduced myself to Ron, who lived three hours away from the prison. After some pleasantries, I walked away, and then fell into conversation with another man, who introduced himself as Tom.

"You know Ron?" Tom nodded toward the first man, who had put his arm around an inmate.

"Just met him today."

"See the guy he's hugging?" I nodded. "Five years ago, that man murdered Ron's only son. Now look at them. How does Ron do it—forgive him, I mean?"

I didn't know.

The first proclamation of the gospel by Jesus was that those who wished to follow him needed to "repent and believe." We are prone to think of "repentance" as giving up sin — and to some degree that is true. However, in the time of Jesus the word would have been more accurately translated, "to radically change the mind, one's way of thinking."

The man visiting his son's murderer every month had "repented." His way of thinking would seem totally foreign to most of us; it makes sense only to those familiar with the gospel message of Jesus: Love your enemies. Forgive seventy times seven. See Christ in the least of his brethren—even in prison.

Sign of Jonah

The people of Jesus' day wanted him to perform a sign to prove that his message was true. Today many of us wish for the same. In reality, these signs are all around us but we are blind to them. Even if we see the sign, it doesn't always convince us. I once attended a healing service where people were literally jumping out of wheelchairs. It didn't make me believe; if anything, I left the service convinced that the healer was a fraud.

In the preceding gospel passage, Jesus called those seeking signs from him evil. They were evil because they refused to acknowledge the many signs that God had already worked in their midst that confirmed that the ministry and teaching of Christ were from God. Even though I am tempted to look with disdain on those who asked for a sign from Jesus in the gospel, I know deep down that I, too, often forget about the many "signs" that God has given me to confirm the truth of Jesus as the Son of God.

In the Gospel of Luke, Jesus promised the "sign of Jonah." This sign is often interpreted as the preaching of repentance: Jonah preached in Nineveh for less than a day before his message produced a radical change in the hearts of the people. By comparison, Jesus had preached for three long years. If pagan Nineveh was so quick to repent, why were those who heard Jesus' message so slow to give up their way of thinking? Earlier in Luke's gospel, Simeon's prophesy may hold the key to this question: "This child is set for the fall and rising of many in Israel, and for a sign that is spoken against" (Luke 2:34).

Jonah preached in Nineveh for less than a day before his message produced a radical change in the hearts of the people. By comparison, Jesus had preached for three long years. If pagan Nineveh was so quick to repent, why were those who heard Jesus' message so slow to give up their way of thinking?

The oldest interpretation of the "sign of Jonah," which is also found in the Gospel of Matthew (16:4) comes from an unfinished commentary on this gospel, penned by an anonymous source dating from the time of the early church fathers. For this nameless wise person, the sign of Jonah was the sign of the cross. His reasoning? St. Paul's letter to the Corinthians, where Paul makes specific reference to the desire for signs among the Jewish people and what he gives them in response—Christ crucified.

Responding to the Sign

What will it take for us to trust in Jesus' message? The cross of Christ can fill people with dread. And yet, it is at the heart of the good news that Jesus preached. It is diametrically opposed to the way the fallen human race thinks; enamored with forbidden fruit, from which it hopes to become "like God." The world shuns the tree that bears the only true Source of life and wisdom. As St. Paul told the Corinthians, "For the word of the cross is folly to those who are perishing, but to us who are being saved it is the power of God" (1 Corinthians 1:18).

To the world, it is foolishness to think that anyone could forgive to the point of embracing his son's killer. As for me, the power of the cross is poignantly revealed in this holy man I once met in a prison in Florida. By embracing the cross, he was able to do exactly what God does when he invites us to his banquet. The cross of Christ either convicts us of murdering God's Son or makes us into a new creation—a being who is truly remarkable to behold.

Steps to Take as You Follow Christ

Ask—Where do I need to repent most in my life?

Seek—Monitor your thoughts and hold them up against the standard of the gospel. Do your love and forgiveness have limitations or conditions? Ask the Lord to teach you true repentance of mind and heart.

Knock—Meditate on 1 Corinthians 1:22–24. How might you experience the power and wisdom of God in the cross by embracing the gospel more completely?

Transform Your Life—Make a daily examination of conscience, paying special attention to your attitudes throughout the day, and asking the Holy Spirit to make you more like Christ.

Day 5

The Cross of Christ Teaches Us . . .
How to Trust and Give Thanks

Every good endowment and every perfect gift is from above, coming down from the Father of lights with whom there is no variation or shadow due to change.

JAMES 1:17

How much more will your Father who is in heaven give good things to those who ask him!

MATTHEW 7:11

Jean's widowed mother gathered her young children around her in their modest Polish home in the 1930s and told them they must pray to God for help. In spite of her hard work, there was no money and no food left in the cupboards. Her mother began the rosary, and the little children huddled close to her, praying that God would come to their aid.

Suddenly they heard a loud commotion outside. Rushing to the window, they saw that the bread man's cart had lost a wheel, causing his cart to tip over. Freshly baked loaves of bread were scattered all over the street. The children rushed out, and the bread man told them to take as much as they could carry; he could do nothing with the bread now that it had been on the ground.

That night before their meal of bread, Jean's family prayed a special blessing in thanksgiving for the way God had provided for them. Years later, Jean realized that there was something for which she was even more thankful: She had a mother whose faith in God was great enough to ask when the straits were dire.

Trusting God for Every Need

Jesus taught his followers to trust that the Father would give them "good things" if they asked. What are those good things? In the story of Jean's widowed mother and her young family, it was a material good, the daily bread they needed to sustain them. For those who are more financially solvent, it may be a spiritual good, like patience or forgiveness. Either way, the cross teaches us what "good things" we need from God.

As we live out the gospel, when we are presented with a cross and we find that we have not the strength to lift it, Christ comes to us as Bread. Like the tipped bread cart, he makes it possible for us to receive the nourishment we need, to participate in his life. His death and resurrection give us Divine Medicine to help us to follow him fully.

What about those too sick to take the medicine? About a year ago I was giving a mission in a parish in the Midwest. On the final night of this mission, which focused on the Mass, the pastor said to me, "What about the Eucharist as Divine Medicine?" Specifically, Father Jerry wondered how those prevented from receiving Communion could receive the Divine Medicine that cures the sinful nature. Long after the mission was over, I continued to ponder his question.

> ✝ *Carry the cross you have been given, and trust that God will give you everything you need.*

What is to be done about those who find themselves unable to participate fully in the Eucharist? First, recognize that the

Eucharist refers to the entire Mass. No one is ever banned from attending the liturgy. There is Divine Medicine in communally declaring our sin before God, hearing his Word proclaimed, and giving thanks to God for all that he has done for us.

If this does not fill the emptiness, find out whether steps can be taken to remove the impediment that is keeping you from the Lord's table. With humility, place yourself before God and ask him to work in your life as you participate as fully as possible in your parish. Go to confession. Guard against pride and anger. Remember, the table the Church gathers around is also an altar of sacrifice. Carry the cross you have been given, and trust that God will give you everything you need.

An Invitation to Ask

The cross cannot be avoided by any of us, and we shouldn't seek to flee from it. Rather, we should learn from it. Wherever we encounter the cross, we discover the "good things" God wants us to request from him. Our Lord promises us that the Father will answer us and give us all that we truly need.

It may require great faith to see the "good" in the things that come our way. The challenge of the cross is to perceive the good even when it causes us discomfort or humiliation. The cross of Jesus did not seem like a "good" thing to those who witnessed the crucifixion. For the followers of Christ, however, the cross is the sign of our salvation; we commemorate "Good Friday" every year because of the great love it represents.

In the Book of Genesis, Joseph endured every conceivable evil at the hands of his family. Later, by faith, he was still able to declare to his brothers, "As for you, you meant evil against me; but God meant it for good, to bring about that many people should be kept alive, as they are today" (Genesis 50:20).

Ask for good things from God and believe that God will give them to you. Believe God wants what is best for you, even when it appears that the opposite is happening. Believe even when people reject you and persecute you. Keep the cross of Christ before you, and you will be reminded that God's ways are not ours, but "that in everything God works for good with those who love him, who are called according to his purpose" (Romans 8:28).

Steps to Take as You Follow Christ

Ask—What do I need from God to follow Jesus more closely?

Seek—As the day progresses, when you find yourself impatient, unloving, judgmental, lustful, or anything that strikes you as against the gospel of Jesus, ask God for the gift that will help you to be more like Christ.

Knock—Meditate on James 1:17. Review the course of your life and try to discern the goodness of God. Spend some time giving thanks to God for how he has led you, even "through the valley of the shadow of death" to this moment.

Transform Your Life—Try to make it a practice to "ask, seek, and knock" in your relationship with God. See that relationship as something that happens with every breath you take. Speak to God often!

Day 6

The Cross of Christ Teaches Us . . . Reconciliation

For the love of Christ controls us, because we are convinced that one has died for all; therefore all have died. And he died for all, that those who live might live no longer for themselves but for him who for their sake died and was raised.

2 CORINTHIANS 5:14–15

But I say to you that every one who is angry with his brother shall be liable to judgment; whoever insults his brother shall be liable to the council, and whoever says, "You fool!" shall be liable to the hell of fire.

MATTHEW 5:22

Sister Mary Agreda refuses to speak to her brother Joe; as far as she is concerned, he died the day that he left the priesthood to marry. Joe is deeply hurt by the fact that his "religious" sister has judged him so harshly. He admits that he has failed in his priestly vocation, but he doesn't understand why his sister has cut him so completely out of her life, especially since the Church has laicized him and recognized his marriage as sacramental.

Even those who seek to do God's will in the most radical fashion sometimes allow their ideals to come between themselves and those around them. I remember being shocked to discover some religious men in a devout community who had not spoken to one another in years—yet gathered in the chapel to pray together every day. This has been happening since the time of Christ, who challenged his followers to conduct themselves by the law of love. As the apostle writes in the first letter of John:

> *If any one says, "I love God," and hates his brother, he is a liar; for he who does not love his brother whom he has seen, cannot love God whom he has not seen.*
>
> 1 JOHN 4:20

We all have our blind spots. When someone disappoints us or harms someone close to us, our inner judge tempts us to punish the offender, to nurse our wounded pride, to exact payment for the perceived offense. At such times, passages of Scripture like this one press like a crown of thorns upon the head, or like nails driven through the feet. It can be tempting to turn a deaf ear to truth; it is so much more immediately gratifying to follow where our fallen passions move us, instead of rushing to reconcile ourselves with a wayward brother or sister.

Nevertheless, Jesus commands us to go. The message of the gospel is unambiguous: Turn the other cheek. Go the extra mile. Offer our cloaks. Judge not. Expect persecution. Love your enemies. If we refuse, we risk becoming like the Pharisees, who knew God's law completely and followed it painstakingly, but shunned God when he appeared in their midst, in the person of Jesus.

Father Alexander Schmemann once observed that modern Christians fall into this same trap: If we make an idol out of our ideology, we miss God even when we meet him face to face. Following Jesus requires a radical change of our attitudes toward others. Our righteousness must *exceed* that of the Pharisees if we are to enter the kingdom of God. On our own power it is impossible, but with God all things are possible.

When Anger Burns, Love Heals

Jesus holds his disciples to a higher standard than what was required by the Law of Moses. We are not to become angry with a brother, referring not just to blood relatives but to the whole human family. According to most commentators, the word that the Revised Standard Version renders as "one who is angry," *raca*, is untranslatable. It was a bad word, not unlike the words in our own language that evoke images of hatred.

There is no mincing of words here, Jesus warns that those who burn in anger will burn in hell. By inflicting anger on another person, we cannot help but harm ourselves. We don't have to like another person's actions; however, in the words of St. Augustine, "You don't love in your enemies what they are, but what you would have them become."

St. Paul told the Corinthians that those who follow Christ are controlled by his love. He died for all, so that all might live. No one, not even the vilest and most evil person imaginable, is excluded from the love of Christ.

When serial killer Ted Bundy was executed in the state of Florida some years ago, one of the news organizations covering his execution interviewed Bundy's mother. Did she still love her son, after all the evil he had done? "Yes," she answered immediately. She didn't like what Ted had done, nor all the pain he had caused his victims and their families, but Ted was her son and she still loved him.

Jesus warns that those who burn in anger will burn in hell.

We tend to forget that God is the Father of every person who has ever existed; unlike our human parents, God will never fail or forget us (see Isaiah 49:15). Because we have experienced this kind of love ourselves, we must show it to our brothers and sisters. It is a debt of love.

When Forgiveness Does Not Come Easy

Once after I had given a talk about forgiveness to a group of people, a woman waited patiently to speak to me. Years before, a man had assaulted her. Unwilling to let the incident become public knowledge, she had never reported the crime, and knew that the man had gone on to harm other women. "I'm afraid to forgive him for what he did to me," she said. "If I forgive, I will be making what he did to me okay."

None of us want to be someone's doormat, or let another person off the hook. However, the cross compels us to live by the light of truth. In this situation, there were two issues that had to be addressed. First, if someone commits a crime, love compels us to turn that person in to the authorities, to hold him accountable for his behavior and to stop him from hurting others. Second, the victim must find a way to come to terms with what has happened; forgiveness does not release the offender, it releases the victim from the power of the offense. Unless she forgives, the offense will become a defining moment in her life and continue to torment her.

In the face of evil, we need help. We need the Holy Spirit to give us courage to love and forgive as Christ did, to confront evil as Christ confronted it, and to let go of anything that hinders us from worshipping the one true God who is the Way, the Truth, and the Life.

Steps to Take as You Follow Christ

Ask— Is there anyone I do not love? In what way can I allow the love of Christ to control me?

Seek—Allow the image of the cross of Christ, the price Jesus paid to redeem all creation, to dominate your thoughts when you find yourself growing angry at someone. Ask the Holy Spirit to empower you to be reconciled to those who have hurt you.

Knock—Meditate on 2 Corinthians 5:14–15. What controls you? What motivates you from the moment of your rising to the point when you take your rest at night? Dwelling on Paul's words, ask the Lord to fill you with his love so that it may be the controlling force in your life.

Transform Your Life—Jesus told his disciples to be reconciled before coming to the altar with their sacrifice. If we carry anger or sin we need to be reconciled to Christ before coming to receive him in the Eucharist. This may mean making contact with people whom we have hurt and asking their forgiveness. We should also go to confession regularly, so that Holy Communion is a true sign of communion with God and all his creatures.

Day 7

The Cross of Christ Teaches Us . . .
How to Love

Beloved, if God so loved us, we also ought to love one another. No man has ever seen God; if we love one another, God abides in us and his love is perfected in us.

1 JOHN 4: 11–12

I say to you, Love your enemies and pray for those who persecute you, so that you may be sons of your Father who is in heaven; for he makes his sun rise on the evil and on the good, and sends rain on the just and on the unjust.

MATTHEW 5: 44,45

No one would have blamed Virginia Cyr if she had been bitter and angry with God for her lot in life. Born with cerebral palsy, she was very young when her mother abandoned the family; a short time later, her father placed Virginia in an orphanage. For the next twenty years of her life she lived in one institution after another, and suffered rejection over and over again. Remarkably, she loved everyone—the poor mother who abandoned her, the people who rejected her, and even a man of the cloth who sexually abused her. What enabled her to so love? The answer is simple: Jesus Christ!

As she wrote in her diary, *Virginia Cyr: God's Little Hobo*: "Each time I left Jesus in these places, I found Him wherever I went. Mother Mary, the intense physical and mental anguish I've been going through recently cannot shake the tremendous peace and joy that fills my heart to overflowing, so that I must laugh, sing, cry, *love all those I see*. O Christ, my Lord, my God, my ALL! Nothing can take me from YOU. Mary, let me find your beautiful Son, ESPECIALLY in the most miserable heart."[1]

The cross that Virginia Cyr carried was precious to her because of the cross of Jesus Christ. Through Jesus' victory on the cross she found hope, joy that she was able to suffer like him, and love for God and all those whom God placed in her path.

The Virtue of Love

Pope John Paul II spoke about this kind of love, the kind that empowers us to love like God, when he said:

> The capacity to love as God loves is offered to every Christian as the fruit of the paschal mystery of the death and resurrection. The Church has expressed this sublime reality by teaching that love is a theological virtue. It is worthy of being called a virtue directly referring to God, and allows the human creature to enter into the circuit of Trinitarian love. In fact, God the Father loves us as he loves Christ, seeing in us His image. This image is, so to speak, painted in us by the Spirit, who like an "iconographer" accomplishes it in time.[2]

When God looks at us, he sees the Son—just as Jesus taught us to see him in the "least of our brethren." Virginia saw the hidden Christ in everyone who crossed her path; this was what enabled her to love. Similarly, as we read in the first letter of John, God's love is within us to the degree that we love other people.

Jesus gave his disciples the power to repair the damage wrought by the forces of evil; they were to preach the good news, to forgive, to heal and announce the kingdom of God. This power is love, and it comes through the Holy Spirit. May the love of God fill our minds and hearts so that we can be vessels that pour that love out in our corner of the world.

The Amazing Power of the Cross

When the love of God is poured out to us through the cross of Christ, it empowers us to do remarkable things in God's name. When Blessed Mother Teresa of Calcutta arose from her prayer before the Blessed Sacrament in the morning, she was empowered to share the love of God with everyone she met, even those who some might consider "unworthy" of her. When the cross spoke to St. Francis at San Daminao, he had no idea that his mission would lead him to preach the love of God to a sultan. After an assassin's bullet failed to take his life, Pope John Paul II was able to embrace his assailant and forgive him.

> God the Father loves us as he loves Christ, seeing in us His image. This image is, so to speak, painted in us by the Spirit, who like an "iconographer" accomplishes it in time.
>
> Pope John Paul II

Where will the cross of Christ take you and me? What will the love of God, as revealed by the cross, empower us to do? Am I willing to allow myself to receive the love of God to such a degree that I cannot contain it? Am I willing to see, despite all appearances, that the stranger before me is the Lord? Before I can answer any of these questions, however, I must ask myself one that is even more important: *Am I willing to die, that all these things might transpire?*

Asking if "I" will do any of these things misses the point. All of us have tried to love God and neighbor with greater fervor, with limited degrees of success. But the "I" must die in order to allow God's Spirit to love through us, both the loving of the

Father and the loving of the Son, as we meet him under all of his guises.

How do we die to ourselves? The cross extends the invitation again and again. We nail our failures and our successes, we make no judgments—like Christ, we abandon ourselves in trust to the Father. We keep "watch" with Christ and live in the expectation of his coming at every moment. Our death on the cross with Christ—something that our Baptism signified but we must daily reclaim—gives us the power to love as Christ did because Christ is within us, when we allow him to be all in all.

Steps to Take as You Follow Christ

Ask—Do I allow God to love through me?

Seek—Keep before you the image of Jesus forgiving those who nailed him on the cross and see everyone with whom you come into contact through Christ. Think about how Christ died for those people and how precious they are as children of God, the same God who loves you.

Knock—Meditate on 1 John 4:11–12. Are there people whom you do not love? Ask God to fill you with his love. What does the Father see in these people that you don't? Ask God to heal you of any painful scars that you still suffer from what others might have done to you. Ask Jesus to touch his wounds from his crucifixion to your own woundedness, that it may become a source of blessing.

Transform Your Life—Put God first in your life. Realize that you can love your spouse, your children, your friends, and your enemies only to the degree that you keep God first. We tend not to expect others to be perfect if we worship the only One who is perfect.

The Cross of Christ Unites...

(WEEK TWO)

And as he [Jesus] was praying, the appearance of . . . his raiment became dazzling white. And behold, two men talked with him, Moses and Elijah, who appeared in glory and spoke of his departure, which he was to accomplish at Jerusalem.

LUKE 9:29–31

THE great reason for the transfiguration was to remove the scandal of the cross from the hearts of his disciples, and to prevent the humiliation of his voluntary suffering from disturbing the faith of those who had witnessed the surpassing glory that lay concealed.

Pope St. Leo the Great

Day 8

The Cross of Christ Unites . . .
The Temporal and Eternal

For we did not follow cleverly devised myths when we made known to you the power and coming of our Lord Jesus Christ, but we were eyewitnesses of his majesty. For when he received honor and glory from God the Father and the voice was borne to him by the Majestic Glory, "This is my beloved Son, with whom I am well pleased," we heard this voice borne from heaven, for we were with him on the holy mountain. And we have the prophetic word made more sure. You will do well to pay attention to this as to a lamp shining in a dark place, until the day dawns and the morning star rises in your hearts.

2 PETER 1:16–19

And Peter said to Jesus, "Lord, it is well that we are here; if you wish, I will make three booths here, one for you and one for Moses and one for Elijah." He was still speaking, when lo, a bright cloud overshadowed them, and a voice from the cloud said, "This is my beloved Son, with whom I am well pleased; listen to him." When the disciples heard this, they fell on their faces, and were filled with awe. But Jesus came and touched them, saying, "Rise, and have no fear."

MATTHEW 17:4–7

Last year my wife and I were in downtown Cleveland when the power suddenly and inexplicably went out all over the city. It was a Thursday afternoon, at the height of rush hour; as we listened to the radio, we discovered that the blackout had affected New York, Detroit, as well as other areas around Lake Erie.

That night, the eve of the Feast of the Assumption, we had planned to attend the Divine Liturgy for the Feast of the Dormition of Mary at a Byzantine Catholic Church in the city. As we gathered at the church with a few other hardy souls, the darkness heightened our awareness of the gleaming candlelight, smoking incense, and jangling bells. Attentively we listened to the reading from the Book of Revelation, "A great portent appeared in the heavens."

Back outside, darkness. The highway was a ribbon of light, streaming both ways, but once we got off the interstate and made our way to the hotel, all was dark again, save a few candles that the hotel staff had placed on some tables.

Everyone at the hotel that night was outside. There was a nervous air to the conversation; everyone wondered when the lights would come back on—and why we were sitting in the darkness in the first place. Finally the hotel staff closed the pool area, and everyone went back to their stuffy hotel rooms. There was no air conditioning, and when I opened a window the air outside did not offer any real relief.

Standing by the window, I peered into the night sky and searched the horizon futilely for signs of light. The bustling city of Cleveland was silent and still, and the darkness continued through the night and into the early morning, a few hours before the natural light of the sun would rise once again.

That experience of darkness brought to mind other images of light and darkness— particularly the Light of God versus the darkness of the world. Peter in his second letter pointed to the Transfiguration of Our Lord as a defining moment, "a light shining in a dark place." Typically, it is only when the lights go out in our lives that we realize how much we need them.

Mel Gibson's movie *The Passion of the Christ* depicted Jesus' Passion and death with overwhelming violence. As gripping as the imagery was, however, it brought to mind scenes I had witnessed on the nightly news that same week. A Jerusalem bus blown up by a terrorist, leaving the streets covered with blood and body parts. An explosion in Iraq that

> *When we feel that inner nudge, that desire to pray, we must pay attention to God's call.*

had left bloody bodies everywhere. Three-year-old Lebanese boys slashed with a sword, their foreheads a bloody mess, as their parents proclaimed a willingness to give up these children to die for their cause. All the violence in our world shrouds it in darkness.

At the Transfiguration, Jesus took Peter, James, and John with him to the top of Mount Tabor to pray. While they were praying, Our Lord's appearance changed, becoming luminous, and the Scriptures tell us: "And behold, two men talked with him, Moses and Elijah, who appeared in glory and spoke of his departure, which he was to accomplish at Jerusalem"(Luke 9:30–31).

Luke's Gospel alone tells us what Jesus talked about with Moses and Elijah: his impending journey to Jerusalem, and his "departure"—that is, his crucifixion—that would be accomplished in that place. Good Friday brought about the first true power outage in recorded history. Long before there was electrical power, we are told, "from the sixth hour there was darkness over all the land until the ninth hour" (Matthew 27:45). This darkness wasn't caused by an incoming thunderstorm; men caused the darkness when they tried to extinguish the Light of the World!

Yet at the moment of his Transfiguration, as he anticipated in prayer the Good Friday that was to come, Our Lord's face was made as bright as the sun. St. Peter's response to this miracle was, "Lord, it is well that we are here!" As they journeyed with Jesus in prayer, every moment of the disciples' lives was an epiphany, an encounter with the Divine. May we, like them, experience that the "light has shone in the darkness."

Prayer That Transforms Life

If we want to learn anything about the Paschal mystery of Jesus' Passion, death, and resurrection here on the mountain of the Transfiguration, we must approach these mysteries on our knees. It all begins with prayer.

Jesus climbed the mountain to be alone with the three disciples, to pray with them. Every effort of prayer begins with an invitation to "come aside." Just as Our Lord called Peter, James, and John to come with him up the mountain, he beckons to us today. When we feel that inner nudge, that desire to pray, we must pay attention to God's call.

It may be difficult to respond to the invitation at times. We need not climb a mountain, at least not literally. However, we do need a place to "come aside." It may be a special corner of our room, or a nearby chapel; no matter where it is, the trip to put oneself into God's presence may seem like scaling the side of a precipice at times. This is to be expected: We are entering a different realm. As Peter, James, and John discovered, in leading them up the mountain Jesus had taken them higher than the geological summit; he had transported them to heaven itself. They were able to witness Moses and Elijah, conversing with Jesus in prayer and blinding light!

As we contemplate the face of Jesus in this "mystery of light," God's purpose for us is revealed. We receive light to illumine our darkness, and strength to persevere as we face our own Good Fridays, when it seems all has been lost. But as we pray before the cross, the Master opens our eyes, enabling us to see the light. Jesus himself comes to us and says, "Rise and have no fear!"

When we receive this foretaste of the kingdom, where "the righteous will shine like the sun" (Matthew 13:43), may we say with St. Peter: "Lord, it is good that we are here!"

Steps to Take as You Follow Christ

Ask—How does the "light" of Christ shine into the darkness of my world?

Seek—At every moment of the day say with St. Peter, "Lord, it is good that we are here!" Realize that when we follow Jesus we see the cross in a new light; we see everything anew where once we could only curse the darkness.

Knock—Meditate on 2 Peter 1:16–19. What is the "power" that St. Peter speaks of as it relates to the Transfiguration? What would happen if you followed his advice to keep the Transfiguration before you as a "lamp shining in a dark place"?

Transform Your Life—Many times we think of our lives as a combination of missed opportunities and mistakes with a few good choices. Applying the lesson of the Transfiguration challenges us to not be so quick to judge negatively but to take a more accepting view of the cross in our own lives. "It is good that we are here" right now, where we are—no matter how it might seem to us at the moment.

Day 9

The Cross of Christ Unites . . .
Those Divided by Sin

For to this you have been called, because Christ also suffered for you, leaving you an example, that you should follow in his steps. He committed no sin; no guile was found on his lips. When he was reviled, he did not revile in return; when he suffered, he did not threaten; but he trusted to him who judges justly. He himself bore our sins in his body on the tree, that we might die to sin and live to righteousness.

1 PETER 2:21–24

Be merciful, even as your Father is merciful.

LUKE 6:36

No doubt you have heard this verse before: "First, they came for the socialists, and I did not speak out because I was not a socialist. Then they came for the trade unionists, and I did not speak out because I was not a trade unionist. Then they came for the Jews, and I did not speak out because I was not a Jew. Then they came for me, and there was no one left to speak."

These are the words of a German Lutheran pastor, Reverend Martin Niemoller. Initially a Nazi sympathizer, he was later declared an enemy of the party and imprisoned in several concentration camps. He only narrowly escaped with his life. In subsequent years he spoke frequently around the world, always ending his talks with a version of this verse.

The original version is the subject of some debate. Some argue that Niemoller spoke of "communists" rather than socialists; others contend that Niemoller said "Catholics." It is likely that Pastor Niemoller changed it himself, to reflect the changing climate of the times, as the diversity of those who had been persecuted by the Nazis was gradually revealed to the world.

The cross of Christ set in motion a reversal of something that began in the Garden of Eden with the sin of our first parents. When God created Eve out of Adam, the man said, *"ishnah"*— "another me." Then the two ate from the tree of Knowledge of Good and Evil, and they immediately noticed that they were naked. Their first impulse was to hide themselves behind fig leaves; the differences between them induced Adam and Eve to distance themselves from one another.

When Jesus rose from the dead, he did not declare a holy war against those who had put him to death. Instead he proclaimed "Peace," and sent his followers to the ends of the earth to preach the gospel, teaching all to believe and trust in him.

Because of sin, this separation grew. As Genesis unfolds sin multiplies, until at the Tower of Babel God confuses the tongues of humans and the division of the people is complete. Complete, that is, until Christ.

Christ Reunites

At the crucifixion, the people were unified in their will that Christ should die. The Romans, representing the civilized world of that time, put Jesus to death; the Chosen People, represented by their leaders, offered up the Son of God in sacrifice.

But from the moment Jesus said to the disciple that he loved, "Behold your mother," and to his Mother, "Behold your son," the separation was over. The divisions that had existed since the time of Adam and Eve began to heal. The gospel of Christ was put in motion by the cross, under which every tribe and nation and people would one day be united. On the day of Pentecost, Babel was reversed. The people heard Peter preach, each in his own tongue. From that moment, the Church was sent throughout the whole world, to reconcile it all to Christ.

St. Paul spells out clearly this reconciliation that Christ has brought about when he says, "There is neither Jew nor Greek ... there is neither male nor female; for you are all one in Christ Jesus" (Galatians 3:28). In Christ the sin of division between people comes to an end.

Mercy to All

Christians are to be forgiving and merciful; we are to live out the unity Christ died to restore. In the early church, outsiders marveled at the followers of Christ because of their love for one another.

Sadly, the unity that was the hallmark of the early Church has been damaged, in some cases seemingly beyond repair. We who are called to be "merciful" stand idly by while our brothers and sisters in other parts of the world are offered up as scapegoats. We who are to share the Good News huddle among our own, contented to preach to the choir. The problem is this: Jesus died for all, so that all might be saved. We who follow Our Lord must live to accomplish his will.

As St. Peter points out, Jesus himself is our example. The treatment that Jesus received on the cross was worse than most of us can even imagine but his message of forgiveness did not change. When Jesus rose from the dead, he did not declare a holy war against those who had put him to death. Instead he proclaimed, "Peace," and sent his followers to the ends of the earth to preach the gospel, teaching all to believe and trust in him.

Unfortunately, the Church has not always been a sign of the unity willed by Jesus. Those who placed their own authority over that of Christ have perpetuated the suffering of Christ through his body the Church. Jesus foresaw this, and warned his disciples as well (see Matthew 13:24–30). Perfect unity won't come until the final harvest, but the "wheat" of the Church needs to embody Jesus' radical message of mercy.

Jesus, I Trust in You!

The Divine Mercy is one of the most popular devotions to arise in the modern church. Based on the written testimony in the famous Diary of St. Faustina, a Polish nun who lived in the early part of the twentieth century, Jesus told Faustina that his mercy was not being preached enough. Jesus asked her to have an image painted, showing rays of red and white light emanating from his heart. Underneath this image are printed five words that reveal the way to avail oneself of that great mercy: "Jesus, I trust in you."

Significantly, St. Faustina's visions occurred shortly before the horrific outrage of the Holocaust, not far from one of the worst concentration camps: Auschwitz. Even then, God was showing his children how to overcome the differences that original sin planted within us. Even then, Our Lord made it clear that the mercy of God is not something we hoard for ourselves, but something we need to extend to others. How many lives might have been saved the horrors of the camps if Jesus' message of mercy had been heard sooner? Whom might we save today?

Steps to Take as You Follow Christ

Ask—Whom do I treat as an outsider in God's kingdom?

Seek—As you go about your daily activities, think about how often you see someone else as "one of them" rather than "one of us." Of course, people are all unique and different. However, the gospel calls us to break down artificial barriers that prevent us from expressing the unity God desires.

Knock— Meditate on 1 Peter 2:21–24 while holding a crucifix in your hands. Think of the example of Jesus on the cross. How might you concretely imitate and model your life on Jesus?

Transform Your Life—Make discernment rather than judgment the goal of your life's decisions. Ask yourself, "What does God want me to do at this moment?" and, "What is God trying to teach me through this?" Strive to be open to his guiding presence. Learn from all whom you meet this day and every day.

Day 10

The Cross of Christ Unites . . .
In Humility

Have this mind among yourselves, which is yours in Christ Jesus, who, though he was in the form of God, did not count equality with God a thing to be grasped, but emptied himself, taking the form of a servant, being born in the likeness of men. And being found in human form he humbled himself and became obedient unto death, even death on a cross. Therefore God has highly exalted him and bestowed on him the name which is above every name, that at the name of Jesus every knee should bow, in heaven and on earth and under the earth, and every tongue confess that Jesus Christ is Lord, to the glory of God the Father.

PHILIPPIANS 2:5–11

He who is greatest among you shall be your servant; whoever exalts himself will be humbled, and whoever humbles himself will be exalted.

MATTHEW 23:11–12

Some years ago, while making a pilgrimage to Medjugorje, a fellow pilgrim shared with me the fact that she struggled with pride. She was attractively dressed, not a hair out of place, even in those primitive surroundings. Yet for all her beauty, she could not help but feel that she was holding herself back from becoming all God wanted her to be.

This woman is not unusual. As we follow the path God has laid out for us, most of us reach a point where we become painfully aware that we are hampering our own spiritual progress. The symptoms may vary—an undisciplined prayer life, a recurring sin, an unwillingness to let go of a past grievance—however, more often than not, the root cause is pride. There are even those who think that they have committed a sin so big that God could never forgive them.

In each of these cases, the antidote is the same: We must be reminded of our rightful place in God's kingdom, so that we think neither less of ourselves nor more of ourselves than we ought. More often than not, that rightful place is restored through an encounter with the cross.

Litany of Humility

I had received a simple litany from my confessor, and gladly passed it on to my new friend. As I did so, I told her what the priest had told me, "This is a prayer that God always answers, usually very quickly."

This litany was written by Cardinal Merry del Val, a great man of the Church who served as Secretary of State under two popes. Cardinal del Val prayed this litany at the end of every Mass he celebrated:

O Jesus meek and humble of heart, *hear me.*
From the desire of being esteemed, *deliver me, Jesus.*
From the desire of being loved, *deliver me, Jesus.*
From the desire of being extolled, *deliver me, Jesus.*
From the desire of being honored, *deliver me, Jesus.*
From the desire of being praised, *deliver me, Jesus.*
From the desire of being preferred to others, *deliver me, Jesus.*
From the desire of being consulted, *deliver me, Jesus.*
From the desire of being approved, *deliver me, Jesus.*
From the fear of being humiliated, *deliver me, Jesus.*
From the fear of being despised, *deliver me, Jesus.*
From the fear of suffering rebukes, *deliver me, Jesus.*
From the fear of being calumniated, *deliver, me, Jesus.*
From the fear of being forgotten, *deliver me, Jesus.*
From the fear of being ridiculed, *deliver me, Jesus.*
From the fear of being wronged, *deliver me, Jesus.*
From the fear of being suspected, *deliver me, Jesus.*

That others may be loved more than I, *Jesus, grant me the grace to desire it.*
That others may be esteemed more than I, *Jesus, grant me the grace to desire it.*
That in the opinion of the world, others may increase, and I may decrease, *Jesus, grant me the grace to desire it.*
That others may be chosen and I set aside, *Jesus, grant me the grace to desire it.*
That others may be praised and I unnoticed, *Jesus, grant me the grace to desire it.*
That others may be preferred to me in everything, *Jesus, grant me the grace to desire it.*
That others may become holier than I, provided that I become as holy as I should,
Jesus, grant me the grace to desire it.

Answered Prayer

That evening our group made the Stations of the Cross up Mt. Krizevac (Cross Mountain), named for the giant concrete cross that had been constructed on the mountaintop by local people to commemorate the 1,900th anniversary of the crucifixion. The climb was treacherous in the best of conditions—well worn, rocky, and steep. That day it was also slippery; it had rained earlier in the day and a steady stream of water flowed down the trail from the top of the mountain.

I spied my friend, who was wearing a beautiful powder-blue jumpsuit, at the second station, where Jesus accepts his cross. As we walked I asked her if she had prayed the litany. She smiled and told me that she had.

When the group reached the seventh station, where Jesus falls a second time, I heard a scream. My friend had slid down the path, her face and clothing covered in mud. Wiping the mud out of her mouth, she came storming up to me and said, "That is the last time I'll pray *that* prayer!"

> "Have a great devotion to the Passion of Our Lord. With peace and resignation put up with your daily troubles and worries. Remember that you are not a disciple of Christ unless you partake of His sufferings and are associated with His Passion."
>
> Cardinal Merry del Val

Humility

At one time in Church history, the Franciscans were given the responsibility of walking before the pope in processions, burning handfuls of flax and chanting, "*Sic transit gloria mundi.*" The flax would disappear almost as quickly as it was ignited, visually affirming the truth of what the monks' intoned: "So goes the glory of the world."

The human race has been fighting the battle against pride since the Fall. Discontent with the lofty position God had given them, they wanted to be just like God—but independent of him. This disordered desire continues to be at the heart of human nature. Only when God's spirit lives within us to the fullest are we able to be most fully human. And the only way to be filled with God's spirit is to empty ourselves of any false sense of who we are, or who we think we have to be. This is the way of humility, what St. Paul calls having "the mind of Christ" (1 Corinthians 2:16).

In the gospels, Jesus warns his disciples against desiring titles and lofty honors. If we achieve greatness in life, as Cardinal del Val did, we must guard against becoming attached to the position or to the glory attached to it. Cardinal del Val gave the following spiritual advice often to those who came to him for counsel:

> Have a great devotion to the Passion of Our Lord. With peace and resignation, put up with your daily troubles and worries. Remember that you are not a disciple of Christ unless you partake of His sufferings and are associated with His Passion. The help of the grace of silence was the only thing that enabled the saints to carry their extremely heavy crosses. We can show our love for Him by accepting with joy the cross He sends our way.

The cross sheds light on the way of humility; it is the path that Christ took and the surest path for us to receive all the blessings that Christ wishes to bestow upon us.

Steps to Take as You Follow Christ

Ask—In what areas of my life do I have the most trouble with pride?

Seek—Say the litany of Cardinal Merry del Val. What parts of the litany do you find it most difficult to say? Take concrete steps to defer to others throughout the day, to die to yourself in little things.

Knock— Meditate on Philippians 2:5–11 and pray that God will give you the mind of Christ. Try to imagine what it was like for Jesus to take upon himself our humanity, with all its limitations. What must it have been like for him to suffer the humiliations of the cross? Now think about your own situation. Are you more like Christ, or our first parents, seeking to "be like God"?

Transform Your Life—Jesus tells his disciples that those who humble themselves will be exalted! Humility is the surest path to real success in the kingdom of God. Pray for humility throughout every day.

Day 11

The Cross of Christ Unites . . .
In Liberty

For I delight in the law of God, in my inmost self, but I see in my members another law at war with the law of my mind and making me a captive to the law of sin which dwells in my members. Wretched man that I am! Who will deliver me from this body of death? Thanks be to God through Jesus Christ our Lord!

ROMANS 7:22–25

The Son of man came not to be served but to serve, and to give his life as a ransom for many.

MATTHEW 20:28

When you read the gospels, you sometimes sense that the disciples of Jesus were not listening to him. He announced his Passion as they made their way to Jerusalem, and they began to squabble over who would get to sit at his right and his left in the kingdom. Whenever Jesus preached the way of the cross, they sought the opposite path. Even when he asked the disciples if they could drink out of the chalice from which he was to drink, they seemed not to catch the full import of what he was saying.

Yet who are we to critique the apostles' inability to comprehend the Lord's message? When we hear of the way of the cross, we filter out the harsh reality of the message. As slaves to pleasure, we flee when faced with the cross or offered the drink from his chalice. Yet God's grace is great; even when we run, we end up right where God wants us.

Order of Redeemers

A young man named Peter fled his native land because a heresy had infected a wide part of the Christian Church there. Another man, Dominic, remained where he was and fought the heresy by founding a religious community, the Dominicans.

Thinking it the best way to preserve his faith, Peter headed south. There he encountered an even greater threat: the Muslim occupation of Spain. Yet this is where God wanted St. Peter Nolasco. When he encountered Christians enslaved by their Moorish captors, Peter knew what the gospel demanded of him. Just as Jesus had come to ransom the many, so St. Peter ransomed those poor souls who had been enslaved because of their faith. Spending all that he had, he ransomed all that he could. In his lifetime he would personally be responsible for the release of more than four hundred captives.

In the Scriptures real enslavement is always seen in terms of our attachment to anything that is not God. Slaves serve a master who has no real right over them. When I do not worship God it is almost as if I open the door to other forces that take hold of me and enslave me.

In 1218 A.D., prompted by a heavenly vision, St. Peter Nolasco founded an order of redeemers. In addition to the traditional vows of poverty, chastity, and obedience, these men took a fourth vow: Should it be necessary, they would offer themselves as a substitute for a captive if it meant that the enslaved might go free. The Mercedarians begged for alms that were used to pay ransom for the enslaved. Sometimes they could not raise enough money and one of the Mercedarians would remain with the captors as a pledge until another could return with the full payment. Many of these brothers were martyred; their lives profoundly touched both the ransomed Christians and the Muslim captors.

Slavery has existed throughout the course of human history; only relatively recently has it been recognized as an affront to human dignity. Even today, there are those who enslave other human beings through political and economic means. Modern followers of Christ still have plenty of opportunities to ransom captive souls.

Freedom from Slavery

In the Scriptures, a person is considered enslaved to the extent that he or she is attached to anything that is not God. "No servant can serve two masters," Jesus says in Luke 16:13. "Either he will hate the one and love the other, or he will be devoted to the one and despise the other. You cannot serve God and mammon."

When God is not master of a person's life, other forces are free to enslave him. A Christian must be especially careful not to become encumbered by lesser "gods," knowing the price Jesus paid to set us free from the bondage of sin. In the passage quoted above from the book of Romans, St. Paul speaks of the horrible effects of this enslavement. *Wretched man that I am! Who will deliver me from this body of death?*

Inevitably, the way of bondage is the way of death. However, even at the moment of death, the liberation of the cross is possible. Two men were crucified with Christ, one on each side of him (the seats that James and John requested). Both prisoners were guilty of the crimes for which they were being executed. However, one admitted his guilt; from his cross, Jesus assured that thief that they would soon be in paradise.

The Way of Freedom

Especially in the United States, freedom is considered a basic human right. And yet, the kind of freedom many people are looking for is just another form of bondage, serving a false god. Some want freedom from a spouse to serve the false god of lust, or freedom from parental authority to serve the false god of self-ishness, or freedom from pain to serve the false god of pleasure.

None of these things constitute true freedom, which comes when we are not enslaved by any of these false gods; instead, we are free to live our lives as God intended. Sadly, this takes a long time for most people to figure out. The realization that they have simply traded one master for another hits some only when they are nailed to a cross of their own making.

I once knew a man who was rather bigoted, a womanizer, and an avowed agnostic. Then he was diagnosed with end-stage bone cancer, with less than a year to live. One day when his life on this earth was nearly over, I sat on the edge of this man's bed. It was like being at the foot of the cross. In those months he had renounced all of his macho ways. He became gentle toward his wife and children, and asked to be baptized into the Catholic faith. I have no qualms with saying that he died a saintly man; he also died a free man! Most of his life he was a slave to what he thought other men wanted to hear, wanted to see—he wasn't himself, he was what he thought he had to be in order to please others. Yet nailed to that harsh cross like the good thief, he was able to steal heaven.

Steps to Take as You Follow Christ

Ask—What continues to enslave me?

Seek—Ask God to point out areas of slavery that still exist in your life. As you go through your day, catch yourself not being true to who you really are, and ask yourself: Who are you serving now?

Knock—Meditate on Romans 7:22–25. Paul talks about delighting in the law of God but finding himself at war with other parts of himself. Spend time reflecting on what delights you about God's law. Ask Christ to save you.

Transform Your Life—Thomas Merton wrote about what he called a person's True Self. Prayer, Merton argued, helps us to discover our True Self: the person God created us to be, totally free from the expectations and demands of others. By contrast, the False Self is enslaved; he cannot be himself, but only what he thinks others want him to be. Starting today, ask God to redeem you from the slavery of the False Self.

Day 12

The Cross of Christ Unites . . .
Those Who Suffer for Justice

I consider that the sufferings of this present time are not worth comparing with the glory that is to be revealed to us.

ROMANS 8:18

But Abraham said, "Son, remember that you in your lifetime received your good things, and Lazarus in like manner evil things; but now he is comforted here, and you are in anguish."

LUKE 16:25

Near the Abbey of Gethsemane in Kentucky is one of the strangest, yet most appropriate settings for a work of art. One has to search for it, and even then it can take some luck to find it. Unlike most art, which is displayed in famous galleries and museums, this work of the famous sculptor Walter Hancock is hidden deep in the Kentucky woods.

A path across the street from the monastery takes you through fields full of wild turkeys that startle easily and fly away noisily, breaking the silence of the place. As you continue through wheat bent down from the wind, and on to a path up a wooded hillside, you have to know what you are looking for or you will likely miss it: a series of statues carved out of dark black stone. The first is of three disciples, exhausted and asleep. About a stone's throw from the first carving is another statue: Jesus in supplication. "Gethsemane" was sculpted to honor the memory of Jonathan Daniels.

Jonathan Daniels was born in Keene, New Hampshire, in March 1939. By the time the civil rights movement was in full swing in the 1960s, he was a seminary student studying at the Episcopal Theological Seminary (now Episcopal Divinity Seminary) in Cambridge, Massachusetts. When in the summer of 1965 Dr. Martin Luther King Jr. called upon divinity students from the north to join him in his march from Selma to the state capitol in Montgomery, Alabama, young Jonathan Daniels traveled south. Tragically, that decision cost him his life. He was shot to death by a deputy sheriff in Haynesville, Alabama. In 1994 the General Convention of the Episcopal Church officially recognized Jonathan Daniels as a martyr.

> Jesus sent his disciples out to heal, to liberate, and to invite others into the kingdom of God. As a follower of Christ, what am I doing for those Jesus sends to me?

I also was born in Keene, New Hampshire, and I grew up hearing the story of the local boy who had traveled south to march against injustice. People weren't always sure exactly why he—why anyone—would venture so far to involve himself in the affairs of other people. Consequently, while Jonathan Daniels was much honored in the Monadnock region of New Hampshire, his motives were not widely understood.

The scene from Gethsemane commemorates Daniel's life perfectly; Daniel understood that following Jesus meant sharing in his Passion. The sleeping disciples, unfortunately, symbolize those of us who are summoned to "watch and pray" but often remain asleep at a distance. Daniel learned his lessons well at the seminary; he went to where Christ was being persecuted. In the end it cost him his life, but the lot of those who suffered was greatly changed by Jonathan Daniel's sacrifice.

When Others Suffer

Jesus tells a story about two dead men: one affluent, the other a beggar. After living a life of luxury, the rich man finds himself suffering in acute pain; he asks Abraham to send Lazarus (the poor beggar) to get him a drink. Even in the afterlife, the rich man thinks that Lazarus should be waiting on him!

Abraham points out the barrier that prevented Lazarus from doing the rich man's bidding in the afterlife. Of course, no such barrier exists among the living. The justice of Lazarus's reward in the afterlife also points to the fact that it is no one's lot to be a beggar in this life; the surplus of some, as Pope John Paul II has often preached, belongs to those in need. While he was alive, the rich man had it within his means to relieve the suffering of Lazarus, but he did nothing. In the mind of the rich man, Lazarus was exactly what God wanted him to be—a beggar. In the next life, the tables were turned: Lazarus was rewarded, and the rich man suffered.

It is a simple message, one that we have heard many times. It also has a touch of irony: In the story, the rich man begs Abraham to send Lazarus back from the dead to warn the rich man's brothers. Abraham predicts that they still wouldn't believe. Notice the reaction of the crowd when Jesus raises Lazarus from the dead: "So the chief priests planned to put Lazarus also to death, because on account of him many of the Jews were going away and believing in Jesus" (John 12:10–11).

Jesus sent his disciples out to heal, to liberate, and to invite others into the kingdom of God. As a follower of Christ, what am I doing for those Jesus sends to me?

God Alone

In the woods of Kentucky, light streams down through the forest cover to the statues frozen in sleep and prayer. Some of it beams upon the observer as well, as though asking him to choose a side. To what group do I belong, the suffering or the sleeping?

Jonathan Daniels chose to speak out for the Lazarus of his day and it cost him his life. However, because of the glory promised, he willingly followed Christ to the cross. I am more like the disciples asleep, overcome with anguish and fear, unable or unwilling to step out for what is right.

At the entrance to the monastery of Gethsemane is a large stone gate. Over the gate are engraved the simple words, "God Alone." Ultimately we all face that moment alone in the garden, when God Alone matters. What a blessing it would be, if every time we are confronted with injustice toward others, we would recognize our turn before the judgment seat of God!

Steps to Take as You Follow Christ

Ask—What does God ask me to do for those who suffer?

Seek—Look for opportunities to help someone who needs it (and who cannot help you back). Stand up for someone who is being brought low.

Knock—Meditate on Romans 8:18. As members of the body of Christ, if one member suffers the entire body suffers. How can you make that suffering redemptive?

Transform Your Life—Read the accounts of the martyrs, those who gave the supreme witness to the gospel with their lives. Many monastic communities read about the lives of the martyrs every day, to inspire those seeking to grow in the Christian life.

Day 13

The Cross of Christ Unites . . .
Us in the Work We Have to Do

Then he showed me the river of the water of life, bright as crystal, flowing from the throne of God and of the Lamb through the middle of the street of the city; also, on either side of the river, the tree of life with its twelve kinds of fruit, yielding its fruit each month; and the leaves of the tree were for the healing of the nations.

REVELATION 22:1–2

Therefore, I tell you, the kingdom of God will be taken away from you and given to a nation producing the fruits of it.

MATTHEW 21:43

Dean wanted to be a Trappist monk. While we were in college, he spent many weekends at a Trappist monastery several hours from our school. These were opportunities for both Dean and the monks of the community to consider whether God was calling Dean to be a Trappist.

Now Trappists are the Marines of monastic life. Until recent times they didn't even speak much. Those of us who knew Dean well found it rather odd that he would think that God was calling him to be a Trappist. Dean loved to talk. He loved to laugh and play jokes on people. He was the most outgoing person in our college class—in a matter of months he knew everyone in the small town where our college was located.

Fortunately the Trappists figured this out, too, and they told Dean that he didn't have a vocation to be a Trappist monk. Unfortunately, he didn't agree with their decision and became very depressed. He felt rejected, but all of us who cared for him were relieved that the monastery had discerned wisely.

Missed Vocations

Many people end up in the wrong job. It is one of the curses of original sin. "Cursed is the ground because of you; in toil you shall eat of it all the days of your life; thorns and thistles it shall bring forth to you; and you shall eat the plants of the field. In the sweat of your face you shall eat bread till you return from the ground, for out of it you were taken; you are dust, and to dust you shall return" (Genesis 3:17–19). I believe that one of the ways this plays out is that we are tempted to take on a career or vocation that simply doesn't match the gifts that God has given to us. As a result, many people find their work a burden, something that does not produce fruit in their lives but rather thorns and thistles.

Jesus compares his coming to that of a son of a wealthy landowner who is sent to obtain produce that has been harvested on the landowner's property. The tenants kill the son, so the landowner gives the vineyard to another group of tenants, who are charged with producing fruit in due season.

The problem is this: Without some help, under the curse of original sin we are no more likely to produce good fruit than those who came before us. But unlike those who came before Jesus, we are not left to our own devices. Jesus identifies himself as the Vine, us as the branches; our ability to produce good fruit is conditioned upon our being "in Christ."

Christian artists throughout history have tied the image of Jesus as the Vine with the image of the Tree of Life, which is mentioned both in the first book of the Bible, Genesis, and the last book of the Bible, Revelation. These artists have perceived a connection between Jesus on the tree of the cross and the Eucharist, where Jesus gives us his Body and Blood under the forms of bread and wine (the fruit of the vine)!

In the Book of Revelation, the Tree of Life is surrounded on either side by the "river of life," a reference to Baptism. It is through this river that we die to ourselves and live for Christ. What is this "self" that has to die in order to gain admittance to the Tree of Life? It is the "false" self, the ego that serves false gods.

What many people never stop to consider is that these false gods can mask themselves as virtuous. This way, it is possible for someone to think he is serving God, when in fact he is really serving some false ideal. How can you tell the difference? A true vocation produces good fruit.

> ✝ We all are the vineyards planted by God. Throughout our lives God sends servants to obtain from us the fruits of our lives. How we respond to them is a good test of whether we are planted in Christ or in our own false self.

About ten years ago, I had an opportunity to make a thirty-day retreat at the Shrine of the North American Martyrs in upstate New York. The grounds of this shrine were covered with statues of every conceivable saint. Since this was a silent retreat, I found myself thinking a lot about the lives of those saints, even talking to the stone figures at times. (They didn't talk back, but obviously I wouldn't make a good Trappist monk either!). As I continued to contemplate their lives, I was struck by the fact that each one was unique: no two saints are alike! Some were extroverts, some were introverts, some were aggressive, some were passive—but they all used the gifts that God had given them in a way that made them remarkable people.

It was clear to those who knew him that my friend Dean had not been not called to be silent monk, withdrawn from the world. Why did he want to be one? He told me once that he felt that in order to be holy; he had to be other than what he was—in his case, that meant being like a monk. Many, many people have been tempted to bury their talents in the name of religion. However, we all are the vineyards planted by God. Throughout our lives God sends servants to obtain from us the fruits of our lives. How we respond to them is a good test of whether we are planted in Christ or in our own false self.

Dean's depression was his own crucifixion. He felt that serving God meant going to a monastery. He was trying to do what he thought was good and right; ironically, it was when he *wasn't* trying to be religious he was doing what was good and right. Dying to ourselves on the cross of Christ means dying to what others expect and being true to what God wants from us.

The Dream that God Gives to Us

In the book of Genesis, Joseph has a dream (see Genesis 37). The dream is Joseph's vocation, what God wants Joseph to do. However, that dream was fulfilled by the way of the cross. Sold into slavery for twenty pieces of silver, Joseph was thrown into jail after being falsely accused of rape. There he interpreted dreams for Pharaoh's cup holder and baker. Years went by before the cup holder remembered Joseph and brought him to Pharaoh's attention. After Joseph was put in charge of Egypt, his brothers appeared and prostrated themselves in front of him—fulfilling Joseph's original dream.

The cross unites our gifts and our mission, the purpose God intends for us to fulfill. It also frees us from our preconceived ideas about how God's will should be done, freeing us to use our gifts for the good of all, so that God's kingdom may come and his "will be done!"

Steps to Take as You Follow Christ

Ask—How can dying to myself help me to know God's purpose?

Seek—Ask others to describe what your gifts are, and where they see you as being most authentic in your life. Resolve to see everyone who crosses your path as the servants that God sends to obtain fruit from the harvest.

Knock—Meditate on Revelation 22:1–2. How has your Baptism changed the curse of original sin in your life into the blessing of the mission that God gives you in Christ? When you receive the Eucharist, imagine that Christ is grafting you to himself, so that his life, his healing, his strength flow through you.

Transform Your Life—Ask Our Lord to reveal to you any areas of your life where you might be serving false gods. Ask him to help you to abandon yourself to God's will in your life in the same way that he did in the Garden of Gethsemane. Believe in God's providential care for you, no matter what has happened in your life in the past or present.

Day 14

The Cross of Christ Unites . . .
God's Mercy and Love

From now on, therefore, we regard no one from a human point of view; even though we once regarded Christ from a human point of view, we regard him thus no longer. Therefore, if anyone is in Christ, he is a new creation; the old has passed away, behold, the new has come. All this is from God, who through Christ reconciled us to himself...

2 CORINTHIANS 5:16–18

This man receives sinners and eats with them.

LUKE 15: 2

I met Frank the first time I visited a Catholic seminary. He stood out from the rest of the men training for the priesthood: He radiated an air of confidence. Of all the guys that I met on that two-day visit, he was the only one who seemed really sure of what he was doing there. I mentioned this to Frank as I was getting ready to leave and it was then that he told me something that has stuck with me from that moment on.

Frank was completing his seventh of the eight years of study required for those in training for the priesthood. Reflecting back on those years and the people that he had met over that period of time, he said, "I've met some of the greatest saints and greatest sinners here. I've also learned that most of the time it is hard to tell which are which."

I thought to myself, Frank is going to make a great priest. But a week after I met him, he left the seminary. There were rumors that a young woman who worked in the kitchen at the seminary refectory was pregnant with his child. Instead of being ordained a priest, he was married during what would have been his eighth year in the seminary.

Judge Not

It is clear from even a casual reading of the gospels that Jesus was judged incessantly: by his family, his disciples, the scribes, the Pharisees, the Sadducees, the Greeks, and the Romans. Some thought Jesus was crazy, some thought him a prophet, some thought him an agitator, some hoped he would be a political liberator or a king; only a select few recognized him as the Son of God. He himself said that people called him a drunkard and a glutton. We need look no further than the inability of the people who encountered Jesus in the flesh to see who he really was, to understand why we shouldn't judge . . . ever.

You might think Frank misled me with his confidence and insight; nothing could be further from the truth. I didn't know then, and I don't know now if he was a saint or a sinner. Neither do you. You may judge him, saying, "Well, he obviously committed a sin by getting the young woman pregnant." But what if Frank wasn't the man responsible for her pregnancy? What if he had simply decided to make a home for her and her child after the child's father abandoned the young woman? What if he sacrificed his vocation for the sake of this child? Why, he could be a great saint, a modern St. Joseph!

That is why Frank's comment has stuck with me for these many years: We just don't know. We do not know the real truth about others, and sometimes we don't even know the truth about ourselves.

A Friend of Sinners

One of the most famous parables of Jesus is that of the Prodigal Son. The son demands his inheritance, then goes off and blows it all. He doesn't come to his senses until he is working in a pigsty.

Jesus tells this parable when he is in the process of being judged as someone who consorts with sinners. The "punch line" of the parable hits home for all of us prodigals: Those who are most likely to come to their senses are those who have experienced the emptiness of a life apart from God. The elder sons really don't see any reason to party; they haven't come to their senses yet.

Who is the greatest sinner in the parable of the Prodigal Son? Could it be the older brother, who is angry that his ungrateful little brother had come home? Often we resent this; we identify more with the elder brother than with the younger. In fact, when I've spoken on this parable it has often angered someone: Someone in their family, like the Prodigal Son, has taken the family's money, only to come back penniless and in search of more.

Our natural human way of looking at things is invariably fallible and has to die. For some of us, that means we're not so bad that God can't forgive us; for others, it means we're not so good that we don't need God's mercy.

Ironically, some Scripture scholars think that in the parable of the Prodigal Son, Jesus is the son who takes the inheritance of the Father — his divine mercy and love — and squanders it on sinners! In the end, the Father is pleased. Once you've heard this way of looking at the parable, it's hard to see it in any other way.

Yes, God's mercy is great; however, to experience it fully always involves a bit of a crucifixion on our part. Our natural human way of looking at things is invariably fallible and has to die. For some of us, that means we're not so bad that God can't forgive us; for others, it means we're not so good that we don't need God's mercy. Most of us are incapable of true objectivity; we have no way of knowing how good we really are or even how bad we are. The cross unites God's love and mercy in us, liberating us to place our trust in him.

St. Paul said, "But with me it is a very small thing that I should be judged by you or by any human court. I do not even judge myself. I am not aware of anything against myself, but I am not thereby acquitted. It is the Lord who judges me" (1 Corinthians 4:3–4). This is trust. It is why sinners flocked to the Lord when he walked the earth, and it is why we sinners flock to Mass, where the Lord feeds us with his Body and Blood.

St. Paul says that anyone in Christ is a new creation. Being in Christ is the key. We hide in Christ. We dwell in Christ. He is our life, our hope, and our salvation.

Divine Mercy provides the perfect anecdote to the poison of sin, "Jesus, I Trust in Thee!" Not in riches, not in the ways of the world, not in my judgments, but in Jesus. Only in God will our souls be at rest.

Steps to Take as You Follow Christ

Ask—When have I judged someone wrongly?

Seek—Do you need to be reconciled to someone in your life? It might be someone in your family, a former friend, an enemy, or even God. Go to confession; through the grace of absolution, seek to trust in God more and more.

Knock—Meditate on 2 Corinthians 5:16–18. What does it mean to be a new creation? If you are a new creation, how are you different from those in the world who are not "in Christ"? How do you view others?

Transform Your Life—See the temptation to judge others or even yourself as a personal invitation to take up your cross and to trust in Christ, the friend of sinners. Pray that God will bless both you and those you might judge. Be quick to show the mercy that God shows to you to others.

The Cross of Christ Transforms . . .

(WEEK THREE)

We all, with unveiled face, beholding the glory of the Lord, are being changed into his likeness from one degree of glory to another; for this comes from the Lord who is the Spirit.

2 CORINTHIANS 3:18

We have died with Christ. We carry about in our bodies the sign of his death, so that the living Christ may also be revealed in us. The life we live is not now our ordinary life but the life of Christ: a life of sinlessness, of chastity, of simplicity and every other virtue. We have risen with Christ. Let us live in Christ, let us ascend with Christ, so that the serpent may not have the power here below to wound us in the heel. Let us take refuge from this world. You can do this in spirit, even if you are kept here in the body. You can at the same time be here and present to the Lord. Your soul must hold fast to him, you must follow after him in your thoughts, you must tread his ways by faith, not in outward show. You must take refuge in him. He is your refuge and your strength.

St. Ambrose, *Flight from the World*

Day 15

The Cross of Christ Transforms . . . How We Worship

Do not be deceived; God is not mocked, for whatever a man sows, that he will also reap. For he who sows to his own flesh will from the flesh reap corruption; but he who sows to the Spirit will from the Spirit reap eternal life. And let us not grow weary in well-doing, for in due season we shall reap, if we do not lose heart.

GALATIANS 6:7–9

But the hour is coming, and now is, when the true worshipers will worship the Father in spirit and truth, for such the Father seeks to worship him. God is spirit, and those who worship him must worship in spirit and truth.

JOHN 4:23–24

John struggled with a common sin of the flesh, and found himself in the confessional line every Saturday afternoon. One Saturday, he arrived after the priest had already left the confessional; an usher had to summon Father Will back to the reconciliation room, which evidently put the priest in a less-than-charitable mood.

John confessed his sin, and the priest said to him, "You come here every week to confess the same sin. I wonder if you are truly sorry and repentant. I want you to think about what St. Paul told the Galatians, 'God is not mocked.'"

For over a year John thought again and again about the priest's warning, and wondered if his struggle with this sin was truly mocking God. When John told me about his situation, I encouraged him to read the rest of the passage in Galatians and to ask himself whether he was trying to overcome this failing by "sowing in the flesh" or by "sowing to the spirit." When he had thought about it for a moment, John realized that all of his efforts to overcome this fault were totally focused on the flesh, on his own ego. In fact, it didn't even seem "holy" to bring such a disgusting sin before God.

John is not unique in his struggle; I don't think I've ever met anyone who isn't in some battle with the flesh. But if we are guilty of mocking God, it is in the same way that the Roman soldiers who mocked Christ were guilty of "mocking" him. They dressed him up as a king with a crown of thorns, a rod for a scepter and a cloak of purple, then they spat upon him and struck him. When you and I call Jesus our King, then serve anything or anyone but him, we *are* mocking him.

In our battles with the flesh, the question we must face is this: Who do we think can save us?

The Samaritan Woman

When Jesus came to the Samaritan woman at the well, he asked her for a drink. When our Lord comes to us, he often asks something of us, too, even when he has an abundance to give us. The asking simply makes us recognize our inability to fulfill our own needs by any means other than him.

So when the Samaritan woman protested at his request, Jesus responded by offering her water that would satisfy all of her thirsts. After some debate, she asked Jesus to give her this water. "Call your husband," he told the woman. "I have none," she replied.

In this exchange between Jesus and the woman, we find the theme again: God is not mocked. "You are right in saying, 'I have no husband,'" Jesus chided her. "For you have had five husbands, and he whom you now have is not your husband." We may play games with others, or try to put on our public façade, but God will not be mocked. He knows us.

Startled by Jesus' revelation, the woman changed the subject: Should she be worshipping in Samaria or Jerusalem? Neither, Jesus answered. "God is spirit, and those who worship him must worship in spirit and truth" (John 4:24).

In the Scriptures, "spirit" refers to a person's entire being; it is the breath of God breathed into the clay of Adam, which animates the human person. It is God's life within us that makes it possible to worship God who is spirit.

When our Lord comes to us, he often asks something of us, even when he has an abundance to give us. The asking simply makes us recognize our inability to fulfill our own needs by any means other than him.

Where Is God?

Those of us who were taught using the *Baltimore Catechism* learned on the opening page the response to the question, "Where is God?"

"God is everywhere."

This question and answer were so familiar to us, we could reply to the question automatically. However, we didn't *act* like we believed it. We tended to think of God being present only when we summoned him or in sacred places like churches and shrines.

At Christmastime a few years ago, a coworker gave me a plaque that reads, *"Vocatus atque non vocatus, Deus aderit"* ("Bidden or unbidden, God is present."). Psalm 139 expresses this truth another way:

O Lord, thou hast searched me and known me!
Thou knowest when I sit down and when I rise up;
   thou discernest my thoughts from afar.
Thou searchest out my path and my lying down,
   and art acquainted with all my ways. . ..
Whither shall I go from thy Spirit?
   Or whither shall I flee from thy presence?

PSALM 139:1–3, 7

Worshipping in spirit and truth, which is the kind of worship that God seeks, involves an intimate dialogue, pouring out our hearts and minds to God at all times. The late Bishop John Sheets used to define the spiritual life as a "dialogic relationship," a fancy way of saying that we are in conversation with God at every moment. Nothing we do is too trivial for God, nothing beneath his notice.

If we truly believed this, our lives would be immediately transformed. Gone forever would be the idea that God doesn't care what we do with our lives. There would be no area of our lives that would be off-limits to God. Because when we worship in spirit and truth, we realize that we live because God's breath is within us, and we live best when we acknowledge the source of every breath we take.

Since the time of early Christianity, there have been forms of prayer that use breathing as a cadence for prayer. The Jesus Prayer and the Rosary, along with various forms of contemplative prayer, are all variations of this type of prayer. The real prayer behind all of these methods is the prayer of surrender: "Into your hands I commend my spirit." This was the prayer that Jesus prayed to the Father from the cross.

As we surrender ourselves to God, we acknowledge him to be our source and ask him to animate our actions according to his will at every moment of every day. The inability to surrender in this way, on the other hand, is often the root problem in our struggles in the spiritual life. When we put God anywhere but at the center of our lives, we deceive ourselves. Life is short and unpredictable, and completely beyond our control.

By surrendering to God, we acknowledge where the control belongs, and place ourselves where we were created to be: In the loving hands of our Father, under his watchful eye.

Steps to Take as You Follow Christ

Ask— What do I do with the life God has "breathed" into me?

Seek—From a prayer posture, concentrate on your breathing. As you inhale, ask God to fill you with the Holy Spirit, to animate your every action to do his will. As you exhale, breathe the name from the core of your being: Jesus. Continue to meditate on him.

Knock—Meditate on Galatians 6:7–9. Reflect on the difference between a living person and a corpse. Are most of your actions, actions of sowing in the flesh or sowing to the spirit? Ask God for patience that you might endure in all things by sowing to the spirit.

Transform Your Life—Make it a habit to pray the prayer of Jesus from the cross whenever you find yourself tempted to do something that you know is not of God: "Father, into your hands I commend my Spirit." This prayer that Jesus has given us is the key to moving from sowing in the flesh to sowing to the spirit.

Day 16

The Cross of Christ Transforms . . . How We See Jesus

Come to him, to that living stone, rejected by men but in God's sight chosen and precious; and like living stones be yourselves built into a spiritual house, to be a holy priesthood, to offer spiritual sacrifices acceptable to God through Jesus Christ.

1 PETER 2:4–5

They rose up and put him out of the city, and led him to the brow of the hill on which their city was built, that they might throw him down headlong. But passing through the midst of them he went away.

LUKE 4:29–30

A Benedictine monk of St. Meinrad Archabbey, Father Cyril Vrablic, always began his homilies with the following quip, "Someday, I'm going to write a book. I haven't written any of the pages yet, but I do have a title and some of the chapters." He would then list off the title and chapters of his mythical book. One title I can still remember some twenty years after first hearing it: *"Saints in heaven have all the glory; saints on earth, that's a different story."*

This title got a lot of laughs because of its simple truth: While we admire people of great sanctity once they are no longer around, they can get on our nerves while they still live among us. Jesus, Scripture tells us, could work no miracles in his hometown because of the lack of faith he encountered among them. When he arose to preach in his local synagogue, the local folks saw only the carpenter's son. They were impressed by his eloquence, but his other claims enraged them to the point that they wanted to kill him. Only then did he work a miracle of sorts, passing through their midst and leaving town.

"I Call You Friends"

Where Father Cyril preached, there was a large image of Christ the Teacher. This image of Jesus appears lofty, severe, and royal. It is hardly the image of Jesus that most of us would have living in the twenty-first century. Since Vatican II, Jesus is most often presented—to both children and adults—as our friend.

Jesus called his disciples friends (see John 15:13–15); they called him "Lord" and "Master." I wonder if this isn't what we ought to be doing. There is something about making Jesus our "friend" that seems to rob him of his divinity and robs us of the power of his presence.

We tend to compartmentalize our friends. When we need something, we tend to go to the friend that is most likely to be able to help us. By making Jesus our "friend," the tendency would be for us to approach him in the same way, to invite him only into areas of our lives that we deem "spiritual." The trouble is, most of us equate "spirituality" with angels and church, not with everyday life. So it is no wonder that, as with the people of Nazareth, the Lord doesn't work any miracles in our midst; we have no trust in him.

Jesus taught his disciples that if they had faith the size of a mustard seed (check your spice rack to see how small a mustard seed is) they could do great things. But it is very likely that our faith, our trust in Christ isn't even that big. We think we know Jesus, when in reality we know only our own image of him.

It saddens me when someone who has been raised a Catholic without actually embracing the faith experiences the power of God as an adult through some other means, often through a different Christian church that is not united with the Church. The first apostles turned the world upside down, healing and preaching and raising the dead in the name of Jesus Christ. How is it that the power of Christ is not so easily recognized in our Church today?

Power Transformed

The Jesus that we encounter in the Gospels is amazing. Confronted with sickness, he heals the sick. Confronted with death, he raises the dead. Confronted with opposition, he silences his opponents.

Then comes his Passion. Suddenly, with the exception of curing the ear of the high priest's servant, Jesus reveals a different way of exercising his almighty power — through weakness! He accepts the cross, along with all the punishment and abuse thrown at him, until all is finished and he commends himself to the Father. After he rises from the dead, the only miracles recorded in the Scriptures are his ability to materialize and disappear from the midst of his disciples.

What happened to the power Jesus exhibited during his ministry? He gave those powers to his disciples. Reading the Acts of the Apostles, you find the disciples of Jesus doing the very same things Jesus did in the Gospels, to the point of powerfully accepting death, exhibited in the stoning of Stephen.

The history of the church is filled with examples of the power of Christ working through those who placed their belief in him. The stories that surround the saints tell of people being healed and of martyrs bravely facing death. Even in our own times, in the United States, there are shrines that exhibit crutches left behind after people were healed by the power of Christ.

Time of Unbelief

Our present time is one of unbelief. The modern church has become like the town of Nazareth. We think we know Christ, and as a result he can work no miracles in our midst. It is time to admit our ignorance of Christ. We should ponder the words, "Is not this Jesus, the son of Joseph, whose father and mother we know? How does he now say, 'I have come down from heaven'?" (John 6:42).

Is the Jesus we believe in the same Divine Person revealed to us in Scripture, or have we created a "kinder, gentler" version? Jesus says to us, "You know me, and you know where I come from. But I have not come of my own accord; he who sent me is true, and him you do not know. I know him, for I come from him, and he sent me" (John 7:28–29). Do we worship the Son of God of Scripture, or a false imposter, a pseudo-Christ?

The Jesus rejected by men is the cornerstone of our faith. Without the real Jesus our faith is weak and powerless; with Jesus the Christ, we are powerful in our weakness. We become living stones — animated by the power of Christ, the Son of the all-powerful God.

Steps to Take as You Follow Christ

Ask—Am I overly familiar with Christ?

Seek—Read the Gospels every day. Encounter Christ as he is presented and try to imagine him in the world today, doing the same acts, confronting unbelief in the modern world.

Knock—Meditate on 1 Peter 2:4–5. Rocks are inanimate objects. It is because they don't move that they make good building blocks. Why, then, does Peter talk about "living stones"? Think about this metaphor and your faith life. In what way does your faith in Christ make you a living stone? Think also about the life of St. Peter; what about his experience of Christ might have led him to come up with this image?

Transform Your Life—There is nothing that exists that can transform our lives more than a relationship with Jesus Christ as he really is—give your life to Christ. Believe, placing all of your trust in his powerful being, and embrace his power in your weakness.

Day 17

The Cross of Christ Transforms . . .
How We Forgive

Be kind to one another, tenderhearted, forgiving one another, as God in Christ forgave you. Therefore be imitators of God, as beloved children. And walk in love, as Christ loved us and gave himself up for us, a fragrant offering and sacrifice to God.

EPHESIANS 4:32–5:2

"You wicked servant! I forgave you all that debt because you besought me; and should not you have mercy on your fellow servant, as I had mercy on you?" And in anger, his lord delivered him to the jailers, till he should pay all of his debt. So also my heavenly Father will do to every one of you, if you do not forgive your brother from your heart.

MATTHEW 18:32–35

A woman once shared with me that she had a problem accepting God's forgiveness in her life. She was a merciful woman who willingly forgave others; she just could not believe that God could forgive her past sins. We met from time to time over the course of two years. After that long period of time, she was finally able to talk about what she had done, and why God couldn't forgive her.

What finally enabled her to reveal her sin was an experience she had that I would call a personal revelation. One night as she walked into her kitchen, stopping at the entrance, she witnessed

Jesus nailed to the cross. He raised his head and looked at her, then vanished from the room. That was it, no words, just a look. Yet that look conveyed love and forgiveness that flooded her heart.

Those of us who grew up with a deep sense of sin may remember our early experiences of confession. In those early days when we were young we confessed that we didn't always obey our parents and that we didn't get along that well with our brothers and sisters. Sometimes we even argued and fought with them. As adults, we can smile at such youthful indiscretions.

In adolescence we commit a different variety of sins. We tend to judge these more seriously because we take ourselves more seriously at this point in our lives. But what we don't realize is that these sins are no different from those we committed as small children: We don't obey our parent, God our Father, and we don't get along with our brothers and sisters; every sin that we commit is in some way against God or neighbor.

Separation from God

The consequence of all sin is spiritual death. We should hate all sin, but some sins can nearly destroy our earthly lives, or greatly alter the path God wishes for us to take. The woman that I mentioned at the beginning of this section had committed such a sin; it could have changed the course of her life and greatly hurt the people she loved. Yet by God's grace, the sin never came to light to those who would have been most affected by it. Even so, her knowledge of that sin became a heavy cross that she carried for over forty years. In that sense, her sin did hurt those that she loved: Though they must have perceived the sadness in her soul, they were never able to relieve her inner pain.

Catholics have always taught that there is a temporal punishment attached to sins, a punishment that remains even when God forgives that sin. In some cases it is easy to understand this temporal punishment: If you rob a bank and get caught, even if God forgives you there will still be a price to pay. If you are caught in adultery and are sincerely sorry, God will forgive you but the damage done to your marriage will be real. Sin is evil because it does bad things to us; just as many physical behaviors can lead to the development of various cancers, so sin leads to our destruction. Eve looked at the forbidden fruit and it looked desirable, but partaking of that fruit made both Adam and Eve terminally ill.

> In the same way that a priest absolves us while making the sign of the cross over us — so it is necessary to trace the sign of God's love in the direction of those who wrong us.

Relief

Though confession alone does not remove the temporal penalty of sin, healing still is possible by God's grace. Prayer, reading the Scripture, giving alms, doing good works all are acts that have had indulgences attached to them by the Church. By obtaining an indulgence, the Christian receives healing from the temporal penalty of even the gravest sins, reducing or eliminating altogether the time of purification needed in purgatory (CCC 1471).

Ideally, the Christian is motivated to perform these spiritual exercises not from fear of punishment but out of love for God. As we read in the preceding passage, St. Paul tells the Ephesians to offer themselves as a spiritual sacrifice with Christ, who has paid the debt of our sins. Seeing Christ on the cross and meditating on his love for us should help us to understand how much God loves us.

St. Therese of the Child Jesus thought of herself as an infant when she prayed. She saw God as her Father, bidding her to come up the stairs, something she made feeble attempts to do with little progress. Finally, she said, the Father would come down and carry her up the stairs. This is the perfect image of prayer: God carries us up to the heavens if we allow him to do so. Yet first we must admit our own powerlessness to achieve the heights to which he calls us, so that he might take us where we would not go.

We need to confess our sins regularly, and accept absolution fully — trusting in God's love more than our failings or our sins. Then we must extend that forgiveness to everyone else in our life, knowing that being forgiven is conditioned upon our forgiving in the same way (see Luke 6:37; Matthew 6:15). Failure to forgive means that we do not fully trust God's forgiveness, as if God might change his mind down the road. Yet God's love is everlasting.

The Ignorance of Sin

The greatest example of forgiveness is that of Jesus, who from the cross forgave those who put him there: "Father, forgive them for they know not what they are doing." Who is the "them" to which Jesus was referring? The "them" is us.

There is great ignorance in every sin willfully committed. If we truly understood the consequences of sin, none of us would have the courage to commit even one. In a moment of clarity we may come to our senses, and realize that by our actions we have "sold innocent blood." Yet even when we have a deep sense of our own ignorance in the sins that we commit against others, we often are unwilling to extend that same possibility to those who sin against us.

Forgiving others is an act of the cross. In the same way that a priest absolves us while making the sign of the cross over us — so it is necessary to trace the sign of God's love in the direction of those who wrong us. By seeing them through the eyes of our

Savior, we may find the courage to offer them the forgiveness that he has offered to us.

Steps to Take as You Follow Christ

Ask—Do I still harbor past sins for which I have not accepted God's forgiveness?

Seek—Go to confession regularly. As part of your examination of conscience, review how you have accepted God's forgiveness for past sins in your life, and review how well you have forgiven others in God's name.

Knock—Meditate on Ephesians 4:32–5:2. St. Paul speaks of us as "beloved children" of God. What does being a child of God require of you? How does it affect the way you treat others, who are also God's children?

Transform Your Life—Let your life be marked by being a forgiver. Realize that when you hold on to something you are making a "god" of it, which closes God out of that part of your life.

Day 18

The Cross of Christ Transforms . . . Law and Love

Owe no one anything, except to love one another; for he who loves his neighbor has fulfilled the law. The commandments, "You shall not commit adultery, You shall not kill, You shall not steal, You shall not covet," and any other commandment, are summed up in one sentence, "You shall love your neighbor as yourself." Love does no wrong to a neighbor; therefore love is the fulfilling of the law.

ROMANS 13:8–10

"Think not that I have come to abolish the law and the prophets; I have not come to abolish them but to fulfill them. For truly, I say to you, till heaven and earth pass away, not an iota, not a dot, will pass from the law until all is accomplished."

MATTHEW 5:17–18

In Fort Myers, Florida, at the end of a beautiful street lined on either side with majestic royal palms is a small neon sign. It looks out of place; it is in front of home in a residential area. The simple sign is lit with green letters: GOD IS LOVE.

The first time I saw this sign, I was visiting a classmate who lived next door to this home. "Is there a church here?" I asked.

"No."

"Why is the sign there, then?"

He told me that the family who had lived in the house for the first half of the twentieth century had only one child, a boy.

When World War II started, the boy was drafted into the military and soon was fighting in Europe. Back home in Fort Myers the man and his wife prayed constantly, asking God to protect their son and bring him back safely.

Tragically, their son was killed in the war. Shortly after the young man's body had been returned for burial, the father erected the sign in front of their home.

The next day as I was making my way back home, I passed the sign again: GOD IS LOVE. Why had that father erected the sign, when his prayer had not been answered as he had hoped? Had the man erected the sign in anger? Had he put it up to mock the love that God was supposed to have for us?

I thought of other families I had known who had suffered similar losses, of parents who came home one day to find their child had been killed in an accident. Under such circumstances, I couldn't imagine anyone erecting a sign with the proclamation GOD IS LOVE.

Jesus said that there was no greater love than to lay one's life down for a friend. That is exactly what the Son of God did, and what he asks of his followers as well.

The sign and its story haunted me, reflecting my own internal struggle. A week later, a thought struck me: "For God so loved the world that he gave his only Son, that whoever believes in him should not perish but have eternal life" (John 3:16). That father was not mocking God at all. Rather, he understood in a way that most of us can't imagine what God had sacrificed, giving an only son so that others might live.

Fulfilling God's Law

Jesus said that he had come not to abolish but to fulfill the law and the prophets. On the cross he said, "It is fulfilled" (John

19:30). Jesus said that there was no greater love than to lay one's life down for a friend. That is exactly what the Son of God did, and what he asks of his followers as well.

St. Paul, who at a glance one might be tempted to think of as someone who was against the "law," gives us the reason grace has supplanted the "law." The love of God, which we experience in our lives as grace, flows into us. That love cannot be contained; it is so great that it spills out and must be spent on others. In love — God's love — the law is fulfilled.

The cross of Christ, which is the most eloquent expression of God's love for us, is also the instrument by which we receive that love: We must die to ourselves so that Christ's love might live within us. "Love one another," Jesus commanded. It is a simple message but complex in practice. How should we express that love?

Love is so misused in our day that it almost has ceased to be a good word. *Caritas,* the Latin word for love, can also be translated as "charity." In order to restore the true meaning of "love," perhaps that is the way we should translate it. God showed *charity* to the world, through his Son. Jesus tells us to have *charity* to one another as he has had *charity* on us.

The charity that we are to show to one another is not sentimental or self-serving. We do not expect those we love — whether ourselves, our parents, our spouses, or other people — to be all-knowing and all-loving. First and foremost, we love other people by not making them "gods." We honor those we love despite their human weaknesses and failings, always reserving a special place for God, who is the only perfect Being worthy of worship. The rest of us poor slobs deserve a fair amount of charity because we know only a little, and are limited in every conceivable way. So when we fail each other it is to be expected.

The Power of the Cross

Good Debt

St. Paul says that the only thing we should owe anyone is love. In our "credit card economy," such an idea is difficult to imagine, but perhaps that makes us better suited to grasp Paul's message. We know all about owing others money, but how indebted are we when it comes to love?

We should start by looking at how much we love God. The faith of the family that erected the GOD IS LOVE sign is remarkable. Most of us are quick to blame God for the horrible things that happen to us. Yet, if you really believe that God is up there just waiting to "get" you, how can you love such a supreme being?

This is not the God Christ revealed to us, the God who suffers with us, who became one of us to rescue us from the powers of evil and destruction. In the Scriptures, death is portrayed as an angel; since death is the result of sin, one might presume a bad angel. The love of God, that is, God's charity for us, is what rescues our loved ones from death and makes eternal life possible. God rescues us from sin and its destructive power. God can make good out of the evil others do and intend for us.

This is why God is worthy of love and why God's love enables us to love others in ways that would be impossible without God's love. No matter what happens to us, we know that God is victorious. The psalmist says "O that today you would hearken to his voice! Harden not your hearts" (Psalm 95:7–8).

Steps to Take as You Follow Christ

Ask—How much do I love God?

Seek—God's love for us and his plans for us are greater than our minds can conceive. Starting today, acknowledge these realities by undertaking acts of trust in God throughout the day. Ask God to fill you with his love. Share God's love with everyone.

Knock—Meditate on Romans 13:8–10. Think about the love you owe to others. Jesus often presents the kingdom of God in terms of parables that speak of a king leaving his servants with talents to share with others. Are you giving of yourself in a way that builds up the kingdom of God?

Transform Your Life—Imitate Christ or one of your favorite saints as you go about your daily activities. Plead with God to enable you to show charity to all you meet. Listen intently to those who speak to you, asking yourself what God might be saying to you through them. Give everyone, including yourself and God, the benefit of the doubt.

Day 19

The Cross of Christ Transforms . . .
Our Lives

The scripture says, "No one who believes in him will be put to shame." For there is no distinction between Jew and Greek; the same Lord is Lord of all and bestows his riches upon all who call upon him. For, "every one who calls upon the name of the Lord will be saved."

ROMANS 10:11–13

When a strong man, fully armed, guards his own palace, his goods are in peace; but when one stronger than he assails him and overcomes him, he takes away his armor in which he trusted, and divides his spoil.

LUKE 11:21–22

Popular folklore holds that when the stock market crashed in 1929, many investors jumped out of windows to their deaths. The reality is that, of the few who did take their lives, most chose various other means. Yet the symbolic nature of those few "jumper" suicides was enough to leave a lasting impression upon a generation of people who saw that putting one's trust in money is a dead-end street.

The same can be said about those who put their trust in pleasure, whether that pleasure is derived from drugs or the abuse of sexuality. Deaths from overdoses and sexually transmitted diseases capture the popular imagination because they resonate with something deep in the human psyche: Although we are tempted to think that more money or pleasure can save us, deep down we know that placing one's trust in them leads to death.

Jesus compares this struggle to a battle. Our line of defense may be strong enough to repel some enemies, but they cannot protect us from the strongest opponent — death. Only Jesus promises immortality; only Jesus can deliver it. The false gods Bacchus, Venus, and Mammon may whisper empty promises into our ears, but they can never save us.

Whom Do I Trust?

The bishop who was responsible for the conversion of St. Augustine said, "Faith means battles. If there are no contests, it is because there are none who desire to contend." What Ambrose meant is that if we find our faith relatively easy, we should look again to see how much faith we really have.

> "Faith means battles. If there are no contests, it is because there are none who desire to contend."
>
> St. Ambrose

St. Peter Chrysologus said, "If you want to party with the Devil, you can't celebrate with Christ." In other words, you and I have to choose. Jesus told his disciples, "He who is not with me is against me, and he who does not gather with me scatters" (Matthew 12:30).

Stories of warrior saints abound. St. Padre Pio wrestled with the devil throughout the night. Similar tales are told of St. John Vianney. St. Francis and St. Benedict are both said to have waged great battles with the flesh. Whether the enemy was physical or spiritual, these holy men and women continued to fight — not by their own resources, but by acknowledging, like Paul, that "when I am weak, then I am strong" (2 Corinthians 12:10). Not one person who trusts in Jesus, says St. Paul, "will be put to shame"; what the Lord promises, he delivers.

Lukewarm Faith

I visited the ruins of Laodicea in 1979 while I was serving in Turkey as a member of the United States Army. Of all the seven churches mentioned in Revelation, the ruins of this city were the most desolate. It was destroyed late in the fifth century AD by a terrible earthquake. My memory is of a wide-open field, with an amphitheater and some graves nearby.

In the Book of Revelation, Jesus warns the apathetic Church of Laodicea:

> "I know your works: . . . because you are lukewarm, and neither cold nor hot, I will spew you out of my mouth. For you say, I am rich, I have prospered, and I need nothing; not knowing that you are wretched, pitiable, poor, blind, and naked. Therefore I counsel you to buy from me gold refined by fire, that you may be rich, and white garments to clothe you and to keep the shame of your nakedness from being seen, and salve to anoint your eyes, that you may see. Those whom I love, I reprove and chasten; so be zealous and repent" (Revelation 3:15–19).

Archbishop Fulton J. Sheen, perhaps the greatest American Catholic preacher of the last century, used to say that these words were addressed especially to those of us who live in the northern hemisphere. When I look at the cross of Christ, I realize he's right: The cross speaks of radical commitment; mine is only lukewarm by comparison.

I often harbor thoughts about grasping at things of the world that might offer some guarantee against whatever impending doom lies in the future.

Who You Gonna Call?

I think it is understandable. We live in a consumer society that constantly tries to sell us a slice of heaven: "enough" life insurance, in case you should die suddenly; a "big enough" plot, so that your loved ones will be able to find you; the "right" drug to help you get more out of sex, enhance your mood, keep your kids in line; the list goes on and on. But in the end, will any of these enticing offers truly save us? Of course not.

The cross of Christ forces us to choose sides, to reorder our priorities. It also transforms our personal crosses and gives us hope: We have on our side someone who is victorious over all enemies, all powers and principalities.

St. Leonard said, "Impress on yourself this great truth: Even if all hell's devils come after you to tempt you, you won't sin unless you want to — provided that you don't trust in your own powers, but in the assistance of God. He doesn't refuse help to those who ask it with a lively faith." God offers us all the help we need in this life, if we avail ourselves of it. As the catchy title tune of the movie *Ghostbusters* asks us: "Who ya gonna call?"

Steps to Take as You Follow Christ

Ask—Do I trust in God?

Seek—Frequently call upon the Lord for his help throughout the day. Life was not intended to be a solitary venture; recognize that God is always present, and is there for us when we call upon him.

Knock—Meditate on Romans 10:11–13. What strikes you in the passage? Dwell on that part and let it enrich your faith in Jesus Christ.

Transform Your Life—Pay attention to the way you think and act throughout the day. What do your actions and thoughts say about what you really trust in? When given choices between what you know God wants for you and what others are asking of you, who wins out? Radically commit to trusting in God and watch your life be transformed in ways that you can't even imagine at this moment.

Day 20

The Cross of Christ Transforms . . .
Our Priorities

In this is love, not that we loved God but that he loved us and sent his Son to be the expiation for our sins. Beloved, if God so loved us, we also ought to love one another. No man has ever seen God; if we love one another, God abides in us and his love is perfected in us.

1 JOHN 4:10–12

And the scribe said to him, "You are right, Teacher; you have truly said that he is one, and there is no other but he; and to love him with all the heart, and with all the understanding, and with all the strength, and to love one's neighbor as oneself, is much more than all the burnt offerings and sacrifices." And when Jesus saw that he answered wisely, he said to him, "You are not far from the kingdom of God."

MARK 12:32–34

A young girl dying of cancer befriended a famous archbishop. The bishop had a soft spot in his heart for children like her; his own niece had been diagnosed and he knew firsthand the agony both the patient and her parents faced. The archbishop had extended a standing invitation to the Protestant chaplain of the children's hospital: If any Catholic child in the cancer ward wanted to see a priest, he should be summoned. So it happened that the archbishop was called to accompany this young cancer patient, Lorraine, in her last months of life.

In time Lorraine came to trust the archbishop, and she shared with him her greatest trial. Her parents were angry with God because of her illness. She had been diagnosed when she was five years old, and had not yet made her First Communion. Would it be possible, she asked her friend, to receive the Eucharist before she died?

After consulting with the parents, the archbishop prepared her personally for her first reconciliation, then celebrated Mass in her hospital room, confirming her and giving her First Communion. She lived only a short while longer.

The archbishop said she had great faith but her constant worry was her parents. No doubt she was now interceding for them, that they might come to know the love that she had experienced in her suffering, that same suffering that had become an obstacle of faith to them.

This is the obstacle of the cross — when Our Lord died on the cross, some left believing that he was the Son of God, others left in utter disbelief. Yet the Scriptures tell us that Jesus' death on the cross was a sign of God's love.

Love of God

When the Scriptures speak of love there are three different words used that are all translated in English as "love." There is *eros*, which is a romantic love; sometimes this word is used for the love that we should have toward God and that God has toward us. There is *philia*, the love of friendship; again, this is used both for the love that God has for us and for the love we are to have for God. Yet the most common form of love, the type of love of which Jesus spoke when he said that we should "love the Lord with our whole being" is *agape*, a sacrificial love

— a tough love, a love that can almost feel like we are being crucified.

In the spiritual life, there are times we find ourselves on a spiritual high, literally in love with God. There are other times we experience God as a trusting friend to whom we open our hearts, and with whom we feel solidarity on our life's journey. Yet for all the other times, there is *agape* — sacrificial love!

Agape love is tough. It's how we love our children who are driving us nuts, how children love difficult parents, or how spouses love each other, even when the other person doesn't respond to our every need. It's the type of love we have for our enemies. It can even be the type of love we have for ourselves when we are immersed in feelings of despair and failure. It is the type of love we are to have for God all the time. Yet most of all, it is the type of love that God has for us. The kind of love that induced him to lower himself to our level, suffer at our hands, and love us through it all.

> ✝ God has already lowered himself to our level, suffered at our hands, and loved us through it all. Jesus is the perfect example of being loved by God and loving God.

The School of the Cross

The cross is the school of love. It transforms how we look at God, the world, and everyone around us. Nailed to the cross with Jesus, we sometimes have faith enough to hear him promise, "This day you will be with me in Paradise." Others simply curse God for not taking them down off of the cross.

If you are graced to be a student of the cross, it is your mission to pray with all of your strength for those who are truants of this school. The love of God compels us to love one another, to carry one another's burdens. Realizing that God alone really matters is the first step to entering the kingdom of God. When that kingdom comes, everyone will acknowledge God's priority. Until then, we live in a world where those who know must tell those who don't, and oftentimes those who know best are the children. Fulton Sheen once said there will be only children in the kingdom, something that we adults might want to reflect upon from time to time.

Steps to Take as You Follow Christ

Ask—How does the cross fit into my stance toward God?

Seek—Acknowledge God's priority in your life, over your heart (all of your emotions), over your understanding (all of your thoughts), and over all of your strength (all of your actions).

Knock—Meditate on 1 John 4:10–12. How does John define "love"? What does the death of Jesus on the cross teach us about God's love? How do we find God's love in all the human suffering that we witness? How can we concretely love one another?

Transform Your Life—Will yourself to love God and everyone else with whom you come into contact today and every day. Think about what it means to truly love other people. Seek to be a sacrificial lover first when it comes to the way you love other people and God.

Day 21

The Cross of Christ Transforms . . . How We See Ourselves

Do you not know that the unrighteous will not inherit the kingdom of God? Do not be deceived; neither the immoral, nor idolaters, nor adulterers, nor sexual perverts, nor thieves, nor the greedy, nor drunkards, nor revilers, nor robbers will inherit the kingdom of God. And such were some of you. But you were washed, you were sanctified, you were justified in the name of the Lord Jesus Christ and in the Spirit of our God.

1 Corinthians 6:9–11

But the tax collector, standing far off, would not even lift up his eyes to heaven, but beat his breast, saying, "God, be merciful to me a sinner!" I tell you, this man went down to his house justified.

Luke 18:13–14

William hit the road when he was twenty; hopping aboard his Harley and setting out on a journey that would take him down many sinful roads. He was living the "high life" of booze, drugs, and promiscuous sex. He worked infrequently; often he would hook up with a rock band and travel throughout the country until the band's tour ended, making just enough money to support his lifestyle. Yet the wild life took its toll on him, and even Bill's friends began to worry that he was on a suicidal path.

It was when William hit bottom that he began, in his words, to be "haunted by the Holy Spirit." The Spirit would suggest a pious thought to him, that he would react to violently, not wanting to hear it. But like a gentle breeze it would come back to him again and again.

One night on a bus, a fellow traveler began to converse with William; in many ways the stranger's life paralleled that of William. Like William, the stranger had also felt haunted by God's Spirit. He produced a Bible from his knapsack and handed it to William, and told him to open it and read the first verse that caught his eye. With some reluctance, William did what his fellow traveler suggested, and opened the Bible to 1 Corinthians 6:9–10. As he read the verse out loud, he realized that he was among those St. Paul indicated were excluded from the kingdom of God.

William closed the Bible and handed it back to the stranger. Then closing his eyes he silently prayed that God would wash him of all his sins and help him to live for God alone from that moment on. When he opened his eyes it was as if the entire world had been transformed. Everything seemed charged with light and energy.

William never looked back. Within a year he was working on a reservation in Canada while studying in a Catholic seminary. Eventually he was ordained a priest in the Ukrainian Catholic Church, and he remains faithful to his vocation to this day as a monk in a Canadian monastery.

William's prayer life now centers on the recitation of the Jesus Prayer: "Lord Jesus Christ, have mercy on me, a sinner." Over and over he prays this prayer on a prayer rope. For him this is no empty exercise but a reminder of how destructive a sinful life is and how glorious the life of grace!

Such Were Some of You

Father William's conversion was sparked by Paul's warning to the Corinthians: "Do not be deceived; neither the immoral, nor idolaters, nor adulterers, nor sexual perverts, nor thieves, nor the greedy, nor drunkards, nor revilers, nor robbers will inherit the kingdom of God." To William's dismay, this passage was a succinct description of the lifestyle of his friends and co-workers, and of the fallen world that he and his friends embraced.

When I taught ethics in a Catholic high school, my students would often argue with me that in order to be a successful person in the world, one had to do many of the very things that Paul lists as barring one from God's kingdom. They were reflecting the "gospel" that had been preached to them every day by our culture, which has so often wrecked young lives. I suspect that many of us have been sold this bill of goods to one degree or another. We have fallen into sinful behavior in order to be a part of the crowd that we are hanging out with; we have sold our souls far too cheaply.

> *Perhaps we need to hold up before us the image of sinful lives, the destruction done both to the individuals and to those around them to generate within us the horror that we should have for committing sin in our lives.*

Paul makes it clear that what saves us is being "washed," "sanctified," and "justified" by Christ and the Spirit. In other words, dying to ourselves in Baptism, crucifying our flesh with Christ on the cross, and living by the Spirit. The self that dies in Baptism is a false self — the fallen self that seeks glory from others rather than from God. We are never truly happy when this fallen self rules our lives.

God's Image

We all have been created in the image of God. As long as we live apart from God's grace, we will never be truly at peace. That is why alcohol and drugs are so much a part of the lives of those whose lives are steeped in sin — and why even the addictions that often trap people can be overcome only by trusting in a higher power, namely God.

Perhaps we need to hold up before us the image of sinful lives, the destruction done both to the individuals and to those around them to generate within us the horror that we should have for committing sin in our lives.

If we are to be transformed into the image that God has created us in, we need to respond to his gospel and realize that in doing so we are rejecting the message preached by the world. This presents us with a cross, but a cross that liberates us from what others think we should be and frees us for the purpose for which God has created us.

Steps to Take as You Follow Christ

Ask—From what do I need Jesus to save me?

Seek—God's forgiveness for your sins. Ask God to transform you into the image of his Son, so that you may be an instrument of God's grace to others.

Knock—Meditate on 1 Corinthians 6:9–11. St. Paul presents a list of those unfit for the kingdom of God. What about each sin alluded to in the list might point to someone worshipping something or someone other than God? Is there a particular sin that you struggle with in the list? How is your life different in Christ?

Transform Your Life—Make a good examination of conscience and plan to go to confession on a regular occasion, perhaps once a month. Try to make your confession sincere, letting go of your attempts to control your own life, and a real surrender to the grace of Jesus Christ. Vow to Christ to trust in his mercy to truly transform your life.

The Cross of Christ Illumines . . .

(WEEK FOUR)

Therefore do not pronounce judgment before the time, before the Lord comes, who will bring to light the things now hidden in darkness and will disclose the purposes of the heart.

1 CORINTHIANS 4:5

THE Lord gives light to the blind. Brethren, that light shines on us now, for we have had our eyes anointed with the eye-salve of faith. His saliva was mixed with earth to anoint the man born blind. We are of Adam's stock, blind from our birth; we need him to give us light. He mixed saliva with earth, and so it was prophesied: "Truth has sprung up from the earth." He himself said: "I am the way, the truth and the life."

St. Augustine, Homilies on John

Day 22

The Cross of Christ Illumines . . . Blindness

"As I made my journey and drew near to Damascus, about noon a great light from heaven suddenly shone about me. And I fell to the ground and heard a voice saying to me, 'Saul, Saul, why do you persecute me?' And I answered 'Who are you, Lord?' And he said to me, 'I am Jesus of Nazareth whom you are persecuting.' Now those who were with me saw the light but did not hear the voice of the one who was speaking to me. And I said, 'What shall I do, Lord?' And the Lord said to me, 'Rise, and go to Damascus, and you will be told all that is appointed for you to do.' And when I could not see because of the brightness of that light, I was led by the hand by those who were with me, and came into Damascus."

ACTS 22:6–11

Jesus said, "For judgment I came into this world, that those who do not see may see, and that those who see may become blind." Some of the Pharisees near him heard this, and they said to him, "Are we also blind?" Jesus said to them, "If you were blind, you would have no guilt; but now that you say, 'We see,' your guilt remains."

JOHN 9:39–41

The most unique Holy Saturday I ever experienced occurred when my wife and I decided to go to a monastery for Holy

Week. Saturday was a rainy day and we decided to go to a nearby spot that was advertised up and down the interstate as the place to visit when you were passing through this part of the country — it was a cave. What better spot to spend Holy Saturday, I reasoned, than under the earth? After all, Jesus' body had lain in a tomb on that first Holy Saturday.

So we drove a few miles away from the monastery and joined a group of other travelers in an out-of-the-way location to descend into the earth and explore one of nature's wonders.

✝ *There are those who would conclude that we live in an age when miracles have ceased, but I know that miracles abound — we just don't recognize them.*

What I remember most about the tour of the cave had little to do with the stalactites or the stalagmites but something else that we experienced once we had gone deep into the cave. The tour guide asked us, "How many of you think you have experienced total darkness?" A few people raised their hands. He then told us that he was going to turn off the artificial lighting that illuminated the cave so that we could experience what the first people who had discovered this cave experienced when their light went out.

There was nothing but total, pitch darkness. I held my hand in front of my face but could see absolutely nothing. I knew that it was there because I could sense it but I could see absolutely nothing, no shadow, no outline — just a horrible darkness.

It was the closest that I have ever come to having some understanding of what it must be like to be totally blind.

In *Pilgrim at Tinker Creek,* in a chapter entitled "Seeing," Annie Dillard wrote about people born blind whose sight was restored by a medical procedure. The reaction of those thus healed wasn't what one might expect. Some wanted to go back to the darkness—they found the light too much. Others enjoyed the gift of vision, but to those who had been in darkness since birth it seemed to them that everything was made of light.

Blinded by the Light

In John's Gospel, Jesus divides the world into two camps: those who encounter his light and have their sight restored, and those who encounter that light and are blinded. Jesus told Nicodemus, "And this is the judgment, that the light has come into the world, and men loved darkness rather than light, because their deeds were evil" (John 3:19).

In John's Gospel, Jesus heals a blind man, who has not only his physical sight restored but also comes to see that Jesus is worthy of worship. The Pharisees who question the blind man refuse to believe, no matter how much evidence is brought forward to prove that Jesus had healed him.

Another Pharisee, Saul of Tarsus, later persecuted the followers of Jesus. While setting out on one such mission, Saul was struck by a light from heaven, and heard the voice of Jesus, the suffering Christ. Saul was blinded on his way to Damascus, where a follower of Jesus healed him. Saul became St. Paul, one of the greatest followers of Christ. The preaching of Paul would focus on the crucified Christ, leading many artists to portray the scene of Paul's conversion as an encounter with a cross of light.

None of the Pharisees, including Saul, thought that persecuting the followers of Christ was evil; in fact, they thought they were doing the will of God. We all risk falling into the same trap. How well do you and I truly see? Do we see everything made of light? Or do we only partially see reality as it is?

A World Made of Light

There have been times in my life when I have called upon God to save or help me, and God has answered in dramatic ways. At first I gave thanks for God's intervention in my life. But with time my inner Pharisee began to question the events: Was God really responsible?

There are those who believe that we live in an age when miracles have ceased, but I know better. Miracles abound — we just don't always recognize them. Those cured of physical blindness perceive the world to be made of light; the same is true of those cured of spiritual blindness. What seemed dark and hopeless suddenly becomes a path to glory. The psalmist reflects this spiritual vision when he prays in perhaps the best-known psalm, "Even though I walk through the valley of the shadow of death, I fear no evil; for thou art with me" (Psalm 23:4).

Today there are eye surgeries that allow people to see clearly without corrective lenses. We need the "surgery of the cross" to restore our vision, allowing us to see the world as God sees it. The person filled with the Light perceives light, even in apparent total darkness. As we read in the Gospel of Matthew: "The eye is the lamp of the body. So, if your eye is sound, your whole body will be full of light; but if your eye is not sound, your whole body will be full of darkness. If then the light in you is darkness, how great is the darkness!" (Matthew 6:22–23).

Lord Jesus, touch our eyes that we might see!

Steps to Take as You Follow Christ

Ask—What would it be like to see everything in God's light?

Seek—Observe the world, expecting to see God at work in it. Put skepticism aside and ask God to enlighten your vision!

Knock—Meditate on Acts 22:6–11. St. Paul believed in God both before and after his experience on the road to Damascus; however, he persecuted the followers of Christ before the experience, while he preached Christ afterward. Has your belief in God been tainted by your nationality, your politics, your upbringing? What blinders might God remove from you to help you to see more clearly his will for you?

Transform Your Life—Be open to the healing of Christ. Never presume that what Jesus has to offer is only for someone else. Allow the cross of Christ to enlighten the path you walk daily, transforming all of your experiences in God's light.

Day 23

The Cross of Christ Illumines . . .
Lag Time

Now faith is the assurance of things hoped for, the conviction of things not seen.

HEBREWS 11:1

At Capernaum there was an official whose son was ill. When he heard that Jesus had come from Judea to Galilee, he went and begged him to come down and heal his son, for he was at the point of death. Jesus therefore said to him, "Unless you see signs and wonders you will not believe." The official said to him, "Sir, come down before my child dies." Jesus said to him, "Go; your son will live." The man believed the word that Jesus spoke to him and went his way.

JOHN 4:46–50

It was a director of religious education who introduced me to St. Therese of the Child Jesus. She was a little apologetic about it; we both had advanced degrees in theology, and people with advanced degrees in anything are inclined to be skeptics. However, she had witnessed a number of miracles that just could not be explained away easily.

She explained the usual "routine" for petitioning St. Therese with a prayer request. First comes a novena, a simple prayer that is prayed for nine days, making a petition known to the saint. St. Therese, who said that she wanted to spend her time in heaven showering roses upon souls, then lets the petitioner know that she has heard the prayer by sending the petitioner a sign — usually of roses. My friend shared that when she had prayed, she would inevitably receive a card with roses, or sometimes an actual bouquet.[3]

I needed a job. So I began praying a novena to St. Therese; three days into the prayer I received an ad for roses in the mail. The first time I threw it out, chalking it up to pure coincidence. I received the same ad again the next day. Therese has a good sense of humor. Miraculously, it seemed, a new job came — but then it didn't work out. On the same day that I was thrown into the unemployment line, I was given a painting of St. Therese holding a bouquet of roses as a gift! The next few months were stressful as I sought a new job, but deep down I knew that St. Therese would not let me down. In the end I ended up exactly where God wanted me, although the journey to arrive there was nothing like anything I could ever have imagined.

> ✝ A common response of Jesus to those who respond to him in faith is to tell them that their faith has healed them. The cross illumines what real faith is; it is the dying of our ego and trusting totally in God, especially when it seems that all is lost.

Lag Time

We have a tendency to think that because the miracles Jesus worked while he was on earth brought immediate results, our prayers should work instantaneously, too. When things don't happen right away for us, our faith wanes and we start to look elsewhere for answers. However, if we look closely at the miracle stories found in the Gospels, we see many instances when Jesus "tests" a petitioner by giving him or her a task to complete before the miracle happens. For example, he instructs the blind man to wash in the pool of Siloam. He sends the royal official home. He tells Peter to cast his net on the other side. In each case, the petitioner is rewarded for carrying his or her cross a little further than he or she would have liked.

The ultimate miracle in the Gospels — the resurrection of Jesus — doesn't take place right away, either. Jesus dies on Good Friday, and then rests in the tomb for the entire Sabbath before rising on Easter Sunday. This "delay" should give us assurance: When we face a cross, we can trust that whether the period between promise and fulfillment is a few days or a few decades, God will respond at the appropriate time.

This does not mean that the wait will be pleasant. The royal official whose son was dying was desperate. Anyone facing similar circumstances knows, we want help and we want it immediately. Being told to go home could have sounded like a rejection, but the royal official had great faith in the power of Jesus to fulfill whatever he promised. To the man's delight, his faith was rewarded; his son was healed at the exact moment that Jesus had told his father, "Your son will live."

Believing Against Appearances

In Matthew's Gospel, when Jesus is on the cross the passersby say to him, "If you are the Son of God, come down from the cross" (Matthew 27:40). That Jesus *doesn't* come down is a mystery that we who follow him must internalize. We trust in him alone; not in appearances, not in immediate results, not according to the scenario we have set up in our own minds. Our Lord is faithful, on his terms and not ours. No matter what the situation, our job is to believe in him.

Jesus commonly responded to those who immediately received their miracles, with no lag time, by telling them that their faith had healed them. The cross illumines real faith, the dying of a controlling ego that corresponds to an act of perfect trust, especially when it seems all is lost. Sometimes the cross brings pain to us personally; other times it involves the pain and suffering of those we love. Faith is difficult precisely because it requires that we trust in God's response before we can perceive anything being done. Once God acts, however, we have a sense that God was guiding us all along.

When our earthly life ceases, we will be welcomed into God's kingdom to the degree that we made him the Lord of our lives. For many of us, that will mean some time along the purgative way, learning to release all of our demands upon God. God has found his rightful place in our hearts when we realize that whatever he wills is best for us.

When we look back over our lives, we often find that every event is intricately interwoven with another, and then another, with bright spots of serendipity when we "just happened" to be in the right spot at the right time at key moments. This realization will deepen the mystery that is life; regardless how long or short our life, our mission and purpose is God's. If he seems slow to respond, look to the cross of Christ, which illumines even the lag time between the promise and the fulfillment.

Steps to Take as You Follow Christ

Ask—Do I trust that God answers all prayer?

Seek—Believe in God even when all appearances suggest that God is not listening to you. Think of Jesus on the cross and his resurrection on the third day.

Knock—Meditate on Hebrews 11:1. How strong is your faith, given this particular definition of faith? Are there prayers that you stop praying because it seems that God is not answering them?

Transform Your Life—Live your life in the assurance of God's love, believing strongly that God desires your salvation. See with eyes of faith all that happens to you in any given day. Learn what it means when the Scriptures proclaim, "Believe and be saved!"

Day 24

The Cross of Christ Illumines . . .
Weakness

Three times, I besought the Lord about this, that it should leave me; but he said to me, "My grace is sufficient for you, for my power is made perfect in weakness." I will all the more gladly boast of my weaknesses, that the power of Christ may rest upon me. For the sake of Christ, then I am content with weakness, insults, hardships, persecutions, and calamities; for when I am weak, then I am strong.

2 CORINTHIANS 12:8–10

"Sir, I have no man to put me into the pool when the water is troubled, and while I am going another steps down before me." Jesus said to him, "Rise, take up your pallet, and walk." And at once the man was healed, and he took up his pallet and walked.

JOHN 5:7–9

Judy met me at the entrance of the church, "Ryan will be healed tonight!" she proclaimed. Judy's beautiful young son had been tragically injured in a pool accident when he was very young. She brought Ryan to Mass every day. Sitting in his wheelchair, Ryan's six-year-old face had an angelic stare, as though he had been given a glimpse of heaven.

Ryan's mom Judy was a living saint. She worked full-time, took care of Ryan along with her other boys and her husband while faithfully attending Mass every day. She often could be found praying in the church on her way to work or on her way home. Even so, Judy's certitude made me nervous; I worried that if Ryan weren't healed, Judy's faith might be shaken.

I was seated in the church directly opposite Ryan, facing him. When the healing service began, a priest carried a monstrance, blessing those present who were sick; a religious sister with the gift of healing prayed aloud, asking the Lord to heal all of those who were seeking his touch. I became more anxious as the priest got closer to Ryan. Suddenly I found myself wondering: What would I do if Ryan were healed?

This young man had been frozen in this position for the three years I had belonged to this parish. If he suddenly arose, I realized, my entire world would be turned upside down. I literally broke into a sweat as the priest approached Ryan. When he finally stood in front of Ryan, the boy moved his head and looked at the monstrance containing the Blessed Sacrament, the Real Presence of Jesus Christ. Then something totally unexpected happened — I heard a voice! It seemed to come from the Eucharist in the monstrance: "It's okay, I'm trapped too." I thought I saw a smile form on Ryan's face. The healing service continued, and Ryan's peaceful stare returned.

Ryan died a few weeks later. I ran into his mom about a month afterward, and she told me that she felt his death was the miracle: He had left this world peacefully and totally unexpectedly. She was thankful for the years God had given her to spend with her son after his accident.

Taking Up Our Pallet

I think of Ryan when I read the Gospel account of the man near the pool of Bethesda (see John 5:2–15). While the story may seem like just another healing miracle, it shares a slight difference with several other healing stories — the man is instructed to take up his pallet and to walk away with it. Most commentators make no mention of this, but it strikes me as significant. Surely Our Lord was concerned about something other than littering the pool by the Sheep Gate.

The command is reminiscent of the Lord's command to his disciples to take up their crosses and to follow him. What the cross and the pallet have in common is that they are signs of weakness. Once the man is healed, the Lord tells him to take up the sign of weakness and to carry it with him. Perhaps he intended the pallet to be a physical reminder that his strength came not from himself, but from God.

Perhaps the greatest power that God gives to any of us is the power to embrace our crutches, our leg braces, whatever our weakness might be — but changed, empowered to carry this weakness in the power of God.

Too often the gospel is preached in a way that makes no allowance for weakness. Much of the scandal in the Church has come not from the weakness of the few clergy who have fallen so much as the inability of their superiors to acknowledge this weakness publicly. In the early church there was a group called "penitents." These were individuals who had fallen in sin and sought reentry into the Church. Though they were welcomed back, they were made to do penance for the rest of their lives — and often wore distinctive garb that manifested to others their weakness.

There is great power in weakness that we all fear. The cross of Christ trapped the Son of God but did not restrain his power. When Our Lord comes to us in the Eucharist, he comes to us in what would appear to be the ultimate sign of weakness, becoming our food, putting himself totally into our hands. There is great power there.

In northern Ohio there is a church dedicated to Our Lady of Sorrows; in the basement is a room containing signs of weakness that have been left behind by those who have experienced the power of God at that shrine. Among whiskey bottles, cigarettes, crutches, and leg braces is a mat that once carried a paralyzed man there — who left empowered by God to walk again.

I suspect that the most powerful stories of healing, however, come from those who were unable to leave anything behind. Their weakness, whatever it was, remained with them; however, they had been empowered to carry their weakness in the power of God. This type of healing often goes unnoticed. Even so, it is the greater healing, because it enables us to share in the cross of Christ, to embrace our weakness in the power of God. For the follower of Christ, weakness need not mean defeat!

Steps to Take as You Follow Christ

Ask—Do I embrace my weakness?

Seek—God's help in carrying your weakness daily. Offer up that weakness in the same way that the Lord offered up his suffering on the cross for the salvation of the world.

Knock— Meditate on 2 Corinthians 12:8–10. St. Paul mentions a "thorn in the flesh" that he was given, that he might not become too elated with the many special gifts that God had given to him. No one is sure what this "thorn" was, though there is speculation that it was an eye problem or even might have been the stigmata (the wounds of Jesus marked on his flesh). Whatever it was, it made Paul uncomfortable, but he realized that in this weakness the power of God was made manifest.

Transform Your Life—Look for ways to embrace the Lord present in the weakness of the world: in the hungry, thirsty, sick, lonely, naked, and imprisoned. Experience the power of God made manifest in what the world considers weak.

Day 25

The Cross of Christ Illumines . . .
Death

But we would not have you ignorant, brethren, concerning those who are asleep, that you may not grieve as others do who have no hope. For since we believe that Jesus died and rose again, even so, through Jesus, God will bring with him those who have fallen asleep.

1 THESSALONIANS 4:13–14

"Truly, truly, I say to you, the hour is coming, and now is, when the dead will hear the voice of the Son of God, and those who hear will live. For as the Father has life in himself, so he has granted the Son also to have life in himself, and has given him authority to execute judgment, because he is the Son of man."

JOHN 5:25–27

As I was writing this book, my friend's son returned unscathed from his tour of duty in the Iraqi War. Many people had prayed for him daily while he served overseas, and rejoiced when he arrived home safely. A few months later came horrible and shocking news: My friend's son had been killed in an automobile accident a few miles from his home. His mother wrote to tell me that it was the most difficult thing she had ever faced. I could not imagine her grief. She ended her brief note with "What to say ..." I understood what she meant: faced with such a tragedy, there was little one could say.

St. Paul instructs the Thessalonians about death so "that you may not grieve as others do who have no hope." Some have misinterpreted this passage, claiming that Christians are not to grieve. Unfortunately, modern funerals often resemble canonizations, minimizing or denying altogether the painful reality of separation that death entails. Instead mourners are forced to put on a "party face," to celebrate death even when the survivors are numb with the shock and pain of their loss.

Grief

The death of a loved one is more like Good Friday than Easter Sunday. The darkness that covered the earth on that first Good Friday points, I believe, to the grief of God at the death of his Son. Though Jesus would rise on the third day, the first day was one of horror, pain, and utter grief for all of creation.

Our Lord is recorded in Scripture as crying three times. In the Garden of Gethsemane (Hebrews 5:7), he prayed with tears; he wept over Jerusalem and prophesied its destruction (Luke 19:41); and Jesus wept at the tomb of Lazarus (John 11:35). The third instance is especially puzzling. Jesus was about to raise Lazarus from the dead. So why did he cry? Were his tears for other senseless deaths that take place at every moment of the day? Or was it because the death and sin Our Lord had come to save us from had not yet been utterly vanquished?

> *The horrible effect of sin is death, the saving effect of the cross is life in Christ. What death takes away from us the saving death of Jesus can take away from death and restore to life.*

There is no doubt that it is human to grieve. However, St. Paul tells us that our grief should not be like the grief of those who have no hope of seeing their loved ones again. Our grief should move us toward assisting our loved ones along their journey toward God — daily remembering them in prayer, asking God to remove any obstacles that might keep them from hearing his voice when he calls their names.

Not of This World

I heard a famous theologian say that the greatest problem within the church today is the subtle secularizing of it. A modern funeral is likely not to mention purgatory, or to offer prayers and Masses for the dead; instead, we observe, "Funerals aren't for the dead but for the living." My, how many have lost the faith in what we are doing! When we participate in the liturgy where the entire body of Christ is present, the poor souls and triumphant saints join us in worshipping the one true God. Together, we offer our sacrifice with Christ to the Father through the Spirit.

Funerals aren't for the dead? To be charitable, one could imagine that such a statement reflects the belief that those who believe in Christ do not die but fall asleep. I have attended some services where such statements have been uttered, but they ring hollow. The loss is all too real.

Our society tends to shield itself from the physical reality of death, something that Archbishop Fulton Sheen called the new taboo. This secular problem has crept into the Church. Whenever we are told not to be sad but to rejoice, that we are an "Easter people" who believe in life, not death — one wonders if these people have ever lost a loved one. Some professional liturgists were angered when the Order for Christian Burial, the official rite of the Catholic Church for funerals, permitted the wearing of black or purple vestments as well as white for Funeral Masses. "It's a step backward," they said. In actuality, it is a step of truth, a step toward Christ.

One of the most powerful images in the movie *The Passion of the Christ* is the sorrowful mother. I think we all can relate to her pain, because it is the pain that we all feel when confronted with the horror of death. How ridiculous would it have been if Mel Gibson had portrayed Mary as happy, telling everyone, "He'll rise on the third day, rejoice now, don't be sad." That would have been sad indeed.

Hope

The modern world fears death. Because we exist in a post-Christian world, the resurrection of the dead is still accepted as fact, yet apart from faith in Christ the resurrection of the dead lacks any scientific basis. No one ever points this out, but it should be before it is too late for those who do not know Christ.

In the Gospel of John, Jesus states clearly that he can give life to the dead. This is the hope of every believer in Christ. At the moment of his crucifixion, Jesus gave life to one of the criminals nailed with him. No such promise is given to the unrepentant thief. Jesus and Paul both make it clear that, while Our Lord is a life giver, he also is a judge. For some, eternal life will lead to eternal hellfire.

My friend's statement, "What to say. . ." is a poignant reminder that the death of any human being causes us to face the ultimate fall of our first parents. It startles us into the reality of the fragile hold we have on our own lives and the lives of those we love. Every present moment is a gift; so is every future hope. We exercise that hope by continuing to pray for our loved ones. If God has welcomed them into his kingdom, our prayers will come back to us. There is great comfort in knowing that this communication goes on — those without faith sense this too and often act upon it.

The Gospel of John tells us that those who "hear his voice" will rise to life (John 5:28). Focusing on the cross of Our Lord helps us to hear his voice. The horrible effect of sin is death; the saving effect of the cross is life in Christ. What death takes away from us, the saving death of Jesus can restore. May we never forget that truth, neither when a loved one dies nor at the hour of our death.

Steps to Take as You Follow Christ

Ask—Who can save me from death?

Seek—Pray for the dead, especially those you have known in life—family, friends, co-workers, and benefactors. When you are at Mass, call to mind those who have died when the priest mentions them in the Eucharistic Prayer.

Knock—Meditate on 1 Thessalonians 4:13–14. Think about how Jesus grieved at the tomb of Lazarus and how he has modeled what Christian grief should look like. How has society's denial of death affected the way people are allowed to grieve in our culture? If people who have died come to mind when you read over this passage, pray for them.

Transform Your Life—An ancient Christian practice is to remember death. This is not a morbid fascination with the inevitable but a clarifying experience, reminding us that our final end need not be death but life with God, and that the shortness of our earthly existence should be focused on doing whatever will build up God's kingdom.

Day 26

The Cross of Christ Illumines . . .
Our Choices

And even if our gospel is veiled, it is veiled only to those who are perishing. In their case the god of this world has blinded the minds of the unbelievers, to keep them from seeing the light of the gospel of the glory of Christ, who is the likeness of God.

2 CORINTHIANS 4:3–4

I do not receive glory from men. But I know that you have not the love of God within you. I have come in my Father's name, and you do not receive me; if another comes in his own name, him you will receive. How can you believe, who receive glory from one another and do not seek the glory that comes from the only God?

JOHN 5:41–44

I have made several pilgrimages to foreign lands. In each case I wanted to visit the sites that had been hallowed by the footsteps of our Lord or the apostles. Even so, I familiarized myself with the laws and customs of my host country. St. Augustine felt that this should always be a concern of followers of Christ. We are pilgrims in this world; while we have a duty to "render to Caesar what is Caesar's," we should never lose sight of the fact that our true citizenship is in the kingdom of God.

Italian theologian Archbishop Bruno Forte has said, "Life is either a pilgrimage or a foretaste of death." Every day of our lives, we are either tracing the Lord's footsteps in hopes of sharing in his resurrection, or awaiting a fateful day of death without hope.

To St. Augustine, these groups of people were like two cities: the City of Man, founded in "the love of self, even to the contempt of God" and the City of God, whose occupants love God above all, and who say to their Creator, "Thou art my glory, and the lifter up of mine head" *(City of God,* Book XIV, Chap. 28).

When our earthly pilgrimage is finished, will we be able to say that we have glorified God during our lives? Or did we seek to be glorified by others?

Every human being must choose between the two destinations, for to turn toward one is to walk away from the other. The choice is simple, said St. Augustine: "Love of self till God is forgotten, or love of God till self is forgotten."

Heavenly Glory

When Jesus came unto his own, the Gospel of John tells us, "His own did not accept him," because they preferred darkness to light. This rejection reached its zenith on the cross, where he was abused physically as well as verbally. They mocked him, chided him, ridiculed him — and yet, he did not respond to their taunts. His focus was on his Father:

"Father, forgive them."

"My God, my God, why. . .?"

"Father, into your hands..."

Throughout his ministry, Jesus demonstrated this single-mindedness; he did not seek out the accolades of the crowds, but the pleasure of the One who sent him. The Gospels also reveal the Father's great pleasure in his Son:

At Jesus' baptism in the Jordan: "This is my Son, in whom I am well pleased. . ."

At the Transfiguration, as the disciples witnessed the appearance of Moses and Elijah with their Master: "This is my beloved Son; listen to him."

And at Calvary, we witness the wordless anguish of a Father for the agony his Son had endured: the ground shook, the sky grew black, and the curtain in the Temple was torn in two. This was the glory and praise that Jesus sought, and that made it possible for him to endure the long journey from the Incarnation to the Cross and Resurrection.

There were temptations along the way. The devil tempted Christ to use his own power, instead of his obedience, to win over all the kingdoms of the world. The people wanted to make him a king when he multiplied the loaves and fishes. When he was called good by anyone, he pointed out that God alone was good. And when he approached the hour of his death, Jesus prayed, "I glorified thee on earth, having accomplished the work which thou gavest me to do; and now, Father, glorify thou me in thy own presence with the glory which I had with thee before the world was made" (John 17:4–5).

When our earthly pilgrimage is finished, will we be able to say that we have glorified God during our lives? Or did we seek to be glorified by others? Will we have accomplished everything that God desired?

Whom Will You Serve?

One of the most telling — and the saddest — indicators of American cultural values, of what we consider most important as a society, is revealed by the number of cosmetic, appearance-enhancing surgeries that are performed every year. I'm not talking about plastic surgery done to correct birth defects or other serious conditions brought about by illness or accident. I mean the number of otherwise healthy people who are willing to go under the knife to lift a little here, tuck a little there. What does it say about a person's mental health, to be so insecure that he or she would risk life and limb, just to look a little younger, a little trimmer, a little closer to some arbitrary cultural ideal? And what does it say about the health of a nation, that those most admired never look a day over thirty?

Those of us who carry the cross of Christ, who see ourselves as pilgrims headed for that City of God, are bound to see things very differently. We give glory to God in all things, and seek God's blessing upon all of our undertakings. We will not content ourselves with some self-serving "spiritual quest" that has more to do with love of self than love of God. We understand that physical beauty is transitional at best. What matters most is to become the person God created us to be; which is to be more like Christ. So we refuse to let ourselves get caught up in some endless cycle of trying to become someone we are not.

When Jesus told the apostles that he must suffer at the hands of the rulers and be crucified, Peter told him that it would never happen. Jesus said to Peter, "Get behind me Satan!" He understood that God's way is not our way — and yet, ultimately it is the only way to eternal life.

The choice is yours: Which road will you choose? And who will be your companion for the journey? Are you going to believe those who pressure you to conform to the self-indulgent values of the City of Man? Or will you take the higher road, bound for the City of God?

Steps to Take as You Follow Christ

Ask—Whom am I trying to please with the actions of my life?

Seek—The glory of God in all things, in all of your actions, in all of your interactions with others.

Knock—Meditate on 2 Corinthians 4:3–4. Does the gospel seem like "good news" to you?

Transform Your Life—Foster a sense of pilgrimage as the model of your life. See yourself as someone walking in the footsteps of Christ. At all times seek to serve God first and to do his will in your life.

Day 27

The Cross of Christ Illumines . . .
The Truth

"Men, what must I do to be saved?" And they said, "Believe in the Lord Jesus, and you will be saved, you and your household."

ACTS 16:30–31

So Jesus proclaimed, as he taught in the temple, "You know me, and you know where I come from? But I have not come of my own accord; he who sent me is true, and him you do not know. I know him, for I come from him, and he sent me." So they sought to arrest him; but no one laid hands on him, because his hour had not yet come.

JOHN 7:28–30

A man went on a pilgrimage to Medjugorje, and encountered a woman who brought a stone to him for inspection. "What do you see?" she asked him.

At first he didn't see anything, he told me later. But he figured that the woman would not have brought the rock to him if there weren't anything of note about it. So he studied it from every angle. Finally, he thought he saw something, "I see Jesus, right here," he said, pointing to several indentations in the stone.

The woman grabbed the stone from his grasp. "It's the Blessed Virgin Mary, you idiot!" And she walked away to show her miraculous stone to another pilgrim.

One of the greatest obstacles to faith is perception, both what we see and what we refuse to see. In the Gospels, those who couldn't believe that Jesus was who he claimed to be usually cited that they "knew" where he came from — they knew his mother and father. Yet Jesus claimed to come from God.

Disbelief

Pick up a news magazine around Christmas or Easter, and you will likely encounter a story about the historical Jesus. These fictional accounts of the life of Jesus are based on the works of scholars who disbelieve anything that purports to be miraculous or prophetic. If Jesus foretells future events, the writers of the so-called historical Jesus claim, that is proof enough that Jesus didn't say it at all; the Gospel writer must have composed it after the fact. Yet disbelief in Jesus' power is nothing new.

Jesus asks the crowd in the Gospel of John, "You know me, and you know where I come from?" (John 7:28). It is clear that they do not know, but before we become too smug, we should remember that the question of Jesus is directed as much at us as it was at those in the Temple. We shouldn't assume to know Jesus very well, either.

When people come to me for spiritual direction, I often pose to them a simple question: "When you pray to God, do you direct the prayer to the Father, the Son, or the Holy Spirit?" Most people answer, "The Son." A few reply, "The Holy Spirit." Not one person has ever said, "The Father." When I pry a little as to why they don't pray to the Father, I usually hear something that reflects their views on authority figures and sometimes their relationship with their earthly fathers.

When the Apostle Philip asked Jesus to show them the Father, Jesus pointed out to Philip that anyone who had seen him, Jesus, had seen the Father. So right away, we come up against a view of Jesus that probably doesn't match our notions. The Triune God is not three gods but one. Jesus is the human face of God, God presented to us in a way that we humans can approach.

Knowledge and Relationship

The Christian Church has always been full of people who thought they knew Jesus. In reality, their image of the Lord reflected more about their own lives than about him. In modern times, we simply discount anything that is revealed about Jesus in the Scriptures that we don't like, and fashion a Jesus in our own image — one who hardly ever has the power to save anyone from anything.

So how are we to come to know the real Christ? As Jesus pointed out, knowledge comes from relationship. Jesus claimed to know the Father because it was the Father who sent him. Communion with God is essential to understanding both God and his purpose for us in this life.

Yet what does it mean to "commune" with God, or to come to an understanding of someone we have never seen with our eyes? We may gain a limited intellectual understanding of who Jesus is and what he did for us on earth by studying the Scriptures, God's revelation to us. A prayerful relationship with Our Lord is also essential. To build a lasting relationship with someone, however, it is not enough to read *about* that person; it is also important to talk *with* him and those closest to him — holy men and women throughout the history of the Church who devoted their lives to serving him and telling others about him.

> *Jesus is the human face of God, God presented to us in a way that we humans could approach.*

Communion with God is abandonment; this is where the cross illumines true knowledge for us. We must cast aside preconceptions of who Jesus *should be* and encounter the living Lord as he *is*. We see this abandonment to God in practice when the Gospels tell us that Jesus was not arrested because "his hour" had not yet come. The "hour of Jesus," (e.g., his passion and death) would not happen until God allowed it to happen. The Scriptures recount different attempts by his enemies to arrest or kill Jesus; yet until the appointed time, they did not succeed. Jesus' whole life was lived in obedience to this understanding.

Similarly, those of us who seek to "know" Jesus must seek him out where he may be found. We need to read the Scriptures, the early Church Fathers, and seek to understand how the Church that he founded continues to manifest his presence in the world today, all the while letting go of who we think Jesus should be so that we might receive the true Christ.

Steps to Take as You Follow Christ

Ask—From whom did I learn what I know about Jesus now?

Seek—Read the Gospels daily to come to a deeper understanding of Jesus. Always begin your reading with a prayer asking God to enlighten you in your endeavor.

Knock—Meditate on Acts 16:30–31. The jailor experiences the power of God's protection over the apostles and wishes to be saved. They tell him what is necessary is to believe. What does it mean to believe? How is belief different than knowledge?

Transform Your Life—Jesus often tells his disciples to watch, to be vigilant. Seek the Lord at all times, in all places. Invite him to be a part of every area of your life. Hold nothing back.

Day 28

The Cross of Christ Illumines . . .
The Way to True Unity

Therefore be imitators of God, as beloved children. And walk in love, as Christ loved us and gave himself up for us, a fragrant offering and sacrifice to God.

EPHESIANS 5:1–2

So there was a division among the people over him. Some of them wanted to arrest him, but no one laid hands on him.

JOHN 7:43–44

One of the most remarkable American Catholics of the last century was a humble Capuchin friar whose name in religion was Father Solanus Casey. Solanus served as a friar in Detroit, in New York, and in his final years in the town of Huntington, Indiana. Born of Irish parents, Solanus did not fare well in the seminary, where he was taught by German-speaking priests in Latin, so while he was ordained a priest, he was never allowed to preach a doctrinal homily or to hear confessions.

Yet God gave Solanus the gift of healing, and people sought him out from all over. When he died in 1957, those who knew him regarded him as a saint. He now is recognized as a Venerable, the last step before being beatified by the Church.

Solanus was the community's porter, the doorkeeper. Today we would call him a receptionist, someone who would greet visitors who came to the friary seeking prayers or material comfort.

Solanus did his job so well that people lined up to have a few moments of his counsel.

People of all faiths would come to him requesting prayers and healings. What Solanus would ask of these seekers was rather unique. He told them to "thank God ahead of time" — in other words, to step out in faith, before any miracle had happened; to act before God as though it already had happened.

The way that he normally asked people to express this thanks to God was for them to sign up to have Masses said by the Capuchin mission society, whether they were Catholic or not. Mass is the perfect "thanksgiving," so it made sense to Solanus that if one were to thank God ahead of time, having Mass said was the perfect way to do this.

People continue to seek Solanus's intercession to this day, and they continue to "thank God ahead of time," with remarkable results.

✝ St. Paul tells us to "walk in love," to offer ourselves up as a sacrifice to God. This means dying to all of those things that we like to focus on that keep us apart and focusing rather on the fact that God is the Father of all of us; we all belong to the same family.

Unity

What Solanus taught is what Jesus practiced. In John's Gospel, before Jesus is arrested and crucified he thanks God, ahead of time. He trusts the Father entirely and he teaches his disciples to do the same.

While the people are divided over Jesus and seek to arrest him, no one is able to lay a hand upon him until he gives himself over to them. He freely gives himself to the Father as the Father gives the Son to the world and as the Spirit will be given by the Father and the Son to those who believe and put their trust in God. The Spirit will unite what sin has divided.

John's Gospel tells us that "they wanted to arrest him," but instead they were *captivated by him*. They were as divided in their purpose as we are when we sin — part of us wants to believe, part of us doesn't. Division is one of the results of the original sin of Adam and Eve — and the cross of Christ is the ultimate sign of division, but ironically in that very cross, Christ will make us one.

Do we see this unity anywhere on earth today? In some ways we are more one now than we were fifty years ago, but in many other ways we are more divided. It is to be expected that the world is this way, because the world will remain fallen until Christ comes again, but it is a great scandal that division exists within the body of Christ — the Church.

We cannot here worry about what someone else can do to undo this damage to the body of Christ, this further tearing apart of his flesh — we can only examine what we are doing to repair the damage ourselves.

That They Be One

Father Solanus Casey was a pious priest who lived in the Church prior to the Second Vatican Council, yet one of the remarkable aspects of his life was how he welcomed people of all faiths to his doorstep. He did not change his belief for anyone; he didn't need to because his faith gave him a command to love everyone and he strove with all his might and God's help to do so. The gifts that God gave to him freely, he shared freely with all of God's creation.

St. Paul understood well the unraveling of original sin that Our Lord's death brought about, God's Spirit reuniting what had been torn apart by sin. He took the good news beyond the Jewish nation and religion that were his own, to the very ends of the earth.

Sadly today the Church is wracked with division, in much the same way as the people were when Christ walked among them: They wanted to arrest him rather than be saved by him. Do we not suffer from the same ailment? Do we want to control Our Lord or be controlled by him?

St. Paul tells us to "walk in love," to offer ourselves up as a sacrifice to God. This means dying to all of those things that we like to focus on that keep us apart and focusing rather on the fact that God is the Father of all of us; we all belong to the same family. It means looking at the division that exists and thanking God ahead of time for bringing about the unity of the kingdom, even when we do not see it.

Jesus' journey to the cross was a walk of love, of giving thanks to God and bringing healing to those who reached out to him. This should be our daily path also.

Steps to Take as You Follow Christ

Ask—Am I focused on unity or division within the body of Christ?

Seek—Give thanks to God ahead of time in your prayers. Think of how Jesus instituted the Eucharist (i.e., "thanksgiving") on the night before he died. When you are at Mass, consciously give thanks to God through Jesus for all that God has done and will do in your life.

Knock—Meditate on Ephesians 5:1–2. How can we imitate God as beloved children? Are there people that we are still divided from? Pray for unity among nations and people of various faiths, and that they may come to know the Savior of mankind, Jesus.

Transform Your Life—Be a thankful person even in the midst of situations where there doesn't seem to be much to be thankful for—think about Solanus Casey and how even though he was thought of as someone who had little to offer in his community, because of his faith, through God he became one of the most revered members of the house. Trust God at all times.

The Cross of Christ
Restores . . .

(WEEK FIVE)

Do not fear what you are about to suffer. Behold, the devil is about to throw some of you into prison, that you may be tested, and for ten days you will have tribulation. Be faithful unto death, and I will give you the crown of life. He who has an ear, let him hear what the Spirit says to the churches. He who conquers shall not be hurt by the second death.

REVELATION 2:10–11

IN former times the blood of goats and the ashes of a calf were sprinkled on those who were unclean, but they were able to purify only the body. Now through the grace of God's Word everyone is made abundantly clean. If we follow Christ closely we shall be allowed, even on this earth, to stand as it were on the threshold of the heavenly Jerusalem, and enjoy the contemplation of that everlasting feast, like the blessed apostles, who in following the Savior as their leader, showed, and still show, the way to obtain the same gift from God. They said; "See, we have left all things and followed you." We too follow the Lord, and we keep his feast by deeds rather than by words.

St. Athanasius

Day 29

The Cross of Christ Restores . . .
Life

But Peter put them all outside and knelt down and prayed; then turning to the body he said, "Tabitha, rise." And she opened her eyes, and when she saw Peter she sat up. And he gave her his hand and lifted her up. Then calling the saints and widows he presented her alive.

ACTS 9:40–41

He cried with a loud voice, "Lazarus, come out." The dead man came out, his hands and feet bound with bandages, and his face wrapped with a cloth. Jesus said to them, "Unbind him, and let him go."

JOHN 11:43–44

John was a fixture at the school where I did graduate studies in theology. Everyone there knew his story. He had once been a successful businessman and in his own words "had it all." Then, like Job, he lost everything. His wife left him for a younger man. His partner embezzled money from the business they co-owned. And John drank more and more until he hit rock bottom.

Alcoholics Anonymous and Jesus had pulled John out of that pit. AA meetings and daily Mass would sustain him for the rest of his life. But John still carried the scars of his past; anyone who took the time to know him soon knew well the cross he carried.

One day I sat behind him in church. At the sign of peace, when we shook hands I noticed a bracelet on his arm. After Mass was over, I asked him about it as we were leaving church. He gave me a closer look, and showed me the Latin inscription: *Memento Viva*, "Remember life." This made me think of the opposite phrase often used in Christian spirituality, *Memento Mori*, "Remember death." I asked him about it.

"My brother told me once, 'All you think about is death. You've got to think about life!' I realized he was right, so I had the bracelet made to remind myself to live."

A Sign of Contradiction

John's bracelet is a message that followers of Jesus need to hear. When we look at the sign of our salvation, the crucifix, we see the God-man dying on it. However, that instrument of death is also a sign of contradiction — that is, a vehicle of life. Just as we look at the crucifix and remember how Jesus rose from the dead, so our focus on the cross challenges us to view apparent defeat from a new perspective. What before Christ we regarded as hopeless, in the year of the Lord is hope-filled. For a time, death was the victor; because of Christ, death shall be defeated.

We see a hint of this at the tomb of Lazarus. Jesus entered into a conversation with Martha, the busy-bodied sister of the dead man, who chided Jesus for not arriving soon enough to save his friend. However, Martha also expressed great faith in his ability to intervene, even at that time.

Jesus acknowledged Martha's active faith. "I am the resurrection and the life; he who believes in me, though he die, yet shall he live, and whoever lives and believes in me shall never die" (John 11:25–26).

Jesus next encountered Mary, the more contemplative sister. Mary fell at the feet of Jesus and cried, like her sister, "If only you had been here." This time Jesus didn't speak directly to Mary; instead he asked the mourners to show him where the body of Lazarus had been entombed. Whereas the more active Martha needed a lot of words, which Jesus gave to her, the more contemplative Mary needed only the presence of Jesus to comfort her. The Lord comes to each of us in the way that best meets our needs; he knows what we need because we were created by him.

The ancient spiritual practice of "remembering death" was a sober reminder to focus on that which is most important: anchoring ourselves to Christ, thereby reigning in our wanton nature that often acts out of a fear of death. By facing death daily, the Christian is oriented toward his or her final end.

The conversations between Jesus and the sisters of Lazarus reflect the earthly concerns of those of us who follow Jesus. Note that Jesus did not dismiss the grief of these two women, but wept along with them. When we are confronted with the plague of illness or death, God does not expect us to brush aside our grief.

Both Martha and Mary saw the death of Lazarus as something that had happened because Jesus was not present. The Bible explains death as the result of the sin of the first humans. God breathes life into the clay that is humanity; when God takes back his breath, we die. The sisters, who perceived Jesus as the Son of God, knew that he had power over life and death.

Jesus proclaimed himself not only as the "resurrection" but also as the "life." When I think of this, I see how my friend John's bracelet pointed directly to Jesus. "Remember life" in essence becomes "Remember Jesus." Keep him present, with you at all times, and you will not experience the deaths that result when we separate ourselves from God, but rather you will hear his voice as he calls you out of the tombs of your own failings, losses, and pitfalls.

The Task of Unbinding

Another aspect to the raising of Lazarus often goes unmentioned. When Lazarus walked out of the tomb, he was still bound by burial cloths. Jesus didn't miraculously remove them but instructed: "Unbind him, and let him go" (John 11:44).

These words of Christ teach us something vital. Jesus gave the Church the power to loose and to bind on earth, and declared that their action would be mirrored in heaven (Matthew 16:19). Here he ordered "them" — presumably the apostles who accompanied him on his journey to Bethany — to unbind Lazarus and to let him go.

When we are called out of our tombs and given new life, the Church plays a role in our continued healing. It was in the Church, my friend John discovered, that he could be loosed and encounter the presence of Jesus. We shouldn't lose sight of that, either. The bumbling disciples of Jesus passed these powers of binding and loosing on through the sacrament of Holy Orders, up to the present day. The men to whom these powers have been entrusted don't always seem Our Lord's most capable agents; even so, he uses them. If we listen to his command spoken through them, we, too, shall find healing.

"Unbind him, and let him go." Too many of us carry with us our past deaths; we don't let them go. What John's brother saw John doing was exactly this: although John had been freed from his drinking and past experiences, he hadn't let them go. Remember life, keep Jesus in mind, unbind whatever else is there, and let it go.

Steps to Take as You Follow Christ

Ask—What still binds me?

Seek—See the restorative power of the cross to see all things made new by the death of Jesus—spend some time allowing your past failings, relationships, and the deaths of loved ones to come forward, and present them to the Lord.

Knock—Meditate on Acts 9:40–41. The early Church continued the ministry of Jesus, as does the Church today. In the raising of Tabitha, we see Peter doing what Jesus did. How much do we act on our faith in Christ when we encounter the results of sin in our lives?

Transform Your Life—Remember life; too often we live in the past. Live for the present moment in Christ.

Day 30

The Cross of Christ Restores . . . Forgiveness

Indeed I count everything as loss because of the surpassing worth of knowing Christ Jesus my Lord. For his sake I have suffered the loss of all things, and count them as refuse, in order that I may gain Christ and be found in him, not having a righteousness of my own, based on law, but that which is through faith in Christ, the righteousness from God that depends on faith; that I may know him and the power of his resurrection, and may share his sufferings, becoming like him in his death, that if possible I may attain the resurrection from the dead.

PHILIPPIANS 3:8–11

Jesus looked up and said to her, "Woman, where are they? Has no one condemned you?" She said, "No one, Lord." And Jesus said, "Neither do I condemn you; go, and do not sin again."

JOHN 8:10–11

There are still places where those caught in adultery face certain death, either through domestic violence or at the hands of civil authorities. "The wages of sin is death" has been a literal truth throughout history and even in the present day. This was true in the time of Jesus as well: In John's Gospel the Pharisees brought the woman caught in adultery to Jesus, hoping he would pronounce the death penalty on her.

In reality, it was Jesus the Pharisees were hoping to trap. If Jesus authorized her execution, they could turn him over to the Romans as someone going against Roman law by putting her to death. If, on the other hand, he simply forgave the woman or said that Moses had taught wrongly, they could proclaim him a false prophet who did not believe in the Torah.

Jesus did neither. He lowered himself to the ground and wrote in the sand. This powerful image calls to mind several moments from the Old Testament. First, the creation of Adam, formed from the earth by his Creator. Was Jesus reminding them of their common humanity and the sinfulness in which they all shared? Or perhaps Jesus was evoking the Prophet Jeremiah, who visited the potter who remade and reworked a vessel of clay into a new vessel. The prophet predicted, "Those who turn away from thee shall be written in the earth, for they have forsaken the LORD, the fountain of living water" (Jeremiah 17:13).

The words of Jesus immediately before his encounter with the adulterous woman tie him even more closely to Jeremiah's prophesy: "He who believes in me, as the scripture has said, 'Out of his heart shall flow rivers of living water'" (John 7:38).

"Without Sin"

Pressed for a decision, Jesus rose from the ground and spoke. "Let him who is without sin among you be the first to throw a stone at her" (John 8:7). If this had happened in recent times, the woman would likely have been buried under a mountain of rock. As Archbishop Sheen was fond of saying, "It used to be that only Catholics believed in the Immaculate Conception of Mary. Now everyone believes that he or she is immaculately conceived and without sin." Some deny any personal failings or sins out of sheer arrogance; others blow themselves up with pride, fearful that they could not be loved if their real self was known with all its weakness.

In the Gospel, neither of these things occurred. The crowd dispersed, no doubt beginning with the wisest. The wise know that they are sinners; only the foolish try to deny it. When the oldest and wisest Pharisees walked away, the others departed as well, thinking to themselves, "Well, if he isn't without sin, surely I'm not."

Soon there was no one there but Jesus and the woman. Jesus did not condemn her, and spoke words of healing and forgiveness to her — and, by extension, to us as well. "Neither do I condemn you; go, and do not sin again" (John 8:11).

This is what God is like, how Jesus reveals God the Father to us. So why do some continue to punish themselves for past sins? Why do others find it impossible to admit their own faults? It is simply because they are listening to the voice of the world and not to the voice of Christ.

We find this pattern of forgiveness throughout the New Testament. When Peter declared himself a sinner, the Lord told him that he would make Peter a fisher of men (see Luke 5:8–10). Even after Peter had denied him three times, Jesus gave Peter leadership over the early Church. "Feed my sheep," Jesus said (John 21:17; Matthew 16:16–19). Paul, who persecuted the Church, came to Christ and was commissioned to preach the gospel. As a youth he followed a route of sin; after his conversion, St. Augustine became one of the greatest evangelists the Church has ever known. St. Francis also alluded to an early life of sin, but when Christ spoke to him from the cross, he set about rebuilding the Church.

The world condemns; Jesus forgives. Whose voice do we listen to, who defines us?

The risen sinner is a powerful witness to the One who took our sins on the cross and rose from the dead. We confess our sins not to be defined by them, but to be freed from their bonds. The world condemns; Jesus forgives. Whose voice do we listen to, who defines us?

Pick up any work of a great saint and you will hear that person say he or she is the greatest of sinners; those of us who are not so saintly are apt to think of this as pious jargon. However, I think there is a greater truth in their claims. The difference between them and us is not in the number of sins they have to confess. The difference is in how they keep from repeating their errors; trusting in Jesus is the only way to "go and sin no more."

Steps to Take as You Follow Christ

Ask—Do I believe in the power of Jesus to forgive?

Seek—Acknowledge your sinfulness before God. Make a daily examination of conscience. In whom are you placing your trust, in Jesus or yourself? Frequently ask God to help you to sin no more.

Knock—Meditate on Philippians 3:8–11. What does Paul mean when he speaks of his faith in Christ? Why would he count everything else as a loss and garbage? How can one become more like Christ in his death?

Transform Your Life—See yourself as no different than the greatest sinner or greatest saint. Potentially, you could be one or the other; the outcome depends more upon the one in whom you place your trust than any personal merit of your own.

Day 31

The Cross of Christ Restores . . .
The Image of God

And the LORD said to Moses, "Make a fiery serpent, and set it on a pole; and every one who is bitten, when he sees it, shall live." So Moses made a bronze serpent, and set it on a pole; and if a serpent bit any man, he would look at the bronze serpent and live.

NUMBERS 21:8–9

"When you have lifted up the Son of man, then you will know that I am he, and that I do nothing on my own authority but speak thus as the Father taught me. And he who sent me is with me; he has not left me alone, for I always do what is pleasing to him."

JOHN 8:28–29

Once when my wife and child were touring a large cathedral in the United States, a famous archbishop passed us by; a high-ranking cardinal, visiting the United States from the Vatican, followed him. The archbishop completely ignored us, but the cardinal stopped and took our baby in his arms, talking gibberish to him. We were moved by the actions of the cardinal, who had taken the gospel to heart.

It is amazing how often Jesus took time to notice someone his disciples had passed by or ignored. In the kingdom of God, the first are last and the last are first. No one exemplified this principle better than Christ himself: the Prince of Heaven became a helpless infant, was raised in obscurity, and died like a criminal. People who have seen Mel Gibson's *The Passion of the Christ* are shocked by the violence. What should shock us more is the idea that the all-powerful God would subject himself to being treated in such a fashion by mere mortals. Yet Jesus said in the Scripture that people would realize that he was from God when men "lifted him up" on the cross.

The way of the cross is the path of humility. So often we seek perfection in how we look, the way we dress, the way we speak, or in what we possess. Jesus told his disciples not to worry about any of these things but to seek God's kingship over them first. Jesus then showed them how to do this. Then he took up his cross and invited them to follow.

It is in those who accept that invitation that the divine image is most perfectly restored. When Blessed Mother Teresa would visit one of her communities, the first

We need to look at the cross of Christ to rediscover our soul's inner beauty.

thing she did was to pick up a broom and begin to sweep. Revered during her life as a saint, she sought no special treatment within her community; no task was beneath her. People who met Mother Teresa often remarked at the beauty of her deeply lined face. In her presence, they felt like they were in the presence of God.

In the Image of the Father

Jesus perfectly reveals to us what God is like. By following the way of the cross, we receive a divine "extreme makeover." The path is not an easy one; our ego constantly tries to exert itself over us. Serpents in forbidden trees will whisper of easier paths. However, there is only one way to fulfill what God has planted in our hearts.

"Truly, I say to you, unless you turn and become like children, you will never enter the kingdom of heaven," Jesus warned his disciples (Matthew 18:3). Some people will go amazing lengths to retain their youth. Sadly, these same people will assiduously avoid the spiritual childhood that the gospel demands, the only sure path of eternal life.

Wandering in the desert, the Israelites complained about their lot, and God sent poisonous snakes. As people died around him, Moses prayed to God for mercy. God told Moses to make a fiery bronze serpent and to put it on a pole; all who looked upon this bronze serpent were healed of snakebite. This bronze image foreshadowed the healing tree of Christ; just as Moses had lifted up the serpent in the desert, Jesus told Nicodemus, so would he be lifted up on the cross, and all who would look upon him would be saved.

We need to look at the cross of Christ to rediscover our soul's inner beauty. God loves us so much that he died for us on that cross. As we gaze upon the cross of Christ, what really matters comes to the forefront in our lives, and we find we can let go of all the trivial pursuits that seem to dominate our time and thoughts.

As the psalmist reminds us time and again, what matters is not to seek and be driven by the desire to please other people but to seek what pleases God. We will discover that not by hiding behind fig leaves, as our first parents did, but by coming to him whenever and wherever he calls us.

Steps to Take as You Follow Christ

Ask—What can make me more like Christ in his humility?

Seek—Ask God to reveal to you his purpose for your life. When you do not feel accepted by others, look to the rejection that Jesus endured on the cross and unite your suffering to his.

Knock—Meditate on Numbers 21:8–9. Imagine the people being bitten by serpents, then being healed by staring at the serpent on the pole (which is still the symbol for the medical profession). What do you think healed the people?

Transform Your Life—Learn the acceptance of God. Confess your sins and anything that you think makes you unacceptable to God. Learn to love your physical imperfections and to help others accept theirs and yours.

Day 32

The Cross of Christ Restores . . .
Our Freedom

But now that you have been set free from sin and have become slaves of God, the return you get is sanctification and its end, eternal life. For the wages of sin is death, but the free gift of God is eternal life in Christ Jesus our Lord.

ROMANS 6:22–23

"If you continue in my word, you are truly my disciples, and you will know the truth, and the truth will make you free."... "Truly, I say to you, every one who commits sin is a slave to sin. The slave does not continue in the house for ever; the son continues for ever. So if the Son makes you free, you will be free indeed."

JOHN 8:31,34–36

We live in a time when "truth" is often thought of, even among Christians, as something subjective and up for grabs. This has greatly weakened the ability of the Church to bring the gospel of Christ to the world. Any appeal to the Church as the guardian of truth is met with a litany of accusations against those who have preached one thing and lived another.

The fact that members of the Church remain enslaved by sin, despite the liberating claims of the gospel, can be explained by our inability to "continue in the word" of Jesus. Jesus told his disciples that *if they persisted in their faith,* they would know the truth and it would set them free. Freedom would be theirs only if they picked up their crosses and stepped out in obedience, following Christ even to death.

More than a few people are immersed in lives ruled by addiction — the most evident slavery to sin. Many wish to disassociate sin and addiction, arguing that those who suffer from addictions are not culpable of their acts. However, the effects of sin may be seen both in the life of the addicted person and in the people around him or her. In addition, behavior scientists are demonstrating that those with substance addictions to drugs and alcohol often engage in other activities that can be just as destructive. Some studies show a release of certain chemicals in the brain that mimic the high of drugs and alcohol and lead people to engage in other addictive behaviors to reach this "high."

All of this is proclaimed in the teaching of the New Testament, of course, and even the therapy devised to rescue someone from such behavior is biblically based. The Scriptures teach that sin is both destructive and enslaving. The destructive element is not apparent to the human eye — in the opening pages of Genesis, the forbidden fruit was "a delight to the eyes." Unfortunately, by the time the person recognizes his addiction, he is already caught in its deadly grip.

Sin is by nature enslaving, and we cannot free ourselves from it. We can be freed from future bondage only through a "higher power." Jesus offers us this free gift, but we must continue in his Word in order to experience true freedom.

Just Do It

Father Val Peter, executive director of Boys and Girls Town in Nebraska, wrote a book called *Rekindling the Fires: An Introduction to Behavioral Spirituality.* This spirituality is based not on feeling but on truth, a sort of "just do it" approach that encourages others to act on the truth of the gospel in faith, continuing in the Word of Jesus. Father Val believes that over a period of time the "forced" activity becomes more natural. In many ways Father Val's book is a modern version of living the virtues in order to become a virtuous person.

Every parent grieves when they see a child make the same mistakes they once did; what most parents do not realize is that we are still bound by those "blinders." The details change with age, but if we are not serving God, we are still slaves to some other master that in the end will bring us down to the depths of hell

To the person obsessed with anything that is not God, being freed from that "master" seems impossible. Even taking the first steps toward Christ and away from the "master imposter" is painful, indeed a crucifixion. It is impossible to imagine any other way of living. Yet if we allow the words of Jesus to soak into our minds, bringing us to true repentance, we will wonder how we ever could have been so misled.

> ✝ Every parent grieves when they see a child make the same mistakes they once did; what most parents do not realize is that we are still bound by those "blinders."

As the late Orthodox theologian Father Alexander Schmemann once observed, there is a joy in following Jesus that transcends the suffering that is entailed by taking up one's cross:

"In the world you will have tribulation," Jesus warns us (Jn 16:33). Anyone who would in the smallest degree follow the path of Christ, love him and give himself to him, has this tribulation, recognizes this suffering. The cross is suffering. But through love and self-sacrifice this same tribulation is transformed into joy. It is experienced as being crucified with Christ, as accepting his cross and hence taking part in his victory. "Be of good cheer, I have overcome the world" (Jn 16:33). The cross is joy, "and no one will take your joy from you" (Jn 16:22).[4]

In medieval art, the cross of Christ is portrayed as the tree of life, both as a vine (referring to John 15) and as the source of the Eucharist. Angels are depicted as offering the bread and wine, the fruit of the cross, to those who stand at the foot of it. This image points to the alternative to enslavement that Christ offers us: to be fed by him at the foot of the cross, receiving from him what the others falsely promise.

The false gospels lure us with promises of joy and fulfillment — yet in the end they ensnare us, delivering only misery and despair. Sometimes one has to follow these false masters down a long road to discover that truth. By contrast, the path on which Christ leads us appears arduous and dreary, one to be avoided. In reality, it is the path that leads to true joy, for it delivers everything that our hearts desire most.

"Enter by the narrow gate," our Lord urges us. "For the gate is wide and the way is easy, that leads to destruction, and those who enter by it are many. For the gate is narrow and the way is hard, that leads to life, and those who find it are few" (Matthew 7:13–14). Two roads, two gates. Which are you traveling?

Steps to Take as You Follow Christ

Ask—Are there areas of my life where I am still enslaved?

Seek—Persevere in the teaching of Jesus. Experience the joy of the small victories when standing your ground against the enemy, especially when he seeks to seduce you back into the slavery of sin.

Knock—Meditate on Romans 6:22–23. What does it mean to be a slave of God? Are you a free person? If not, what still enslaves you? If so, from what has God freed you?

Transform Your Life—St. Ignatius of Loyola taught that we should make use of created things inasmuch as they aid us in praising, reverencing, and serving God, for that is the purpose of our existence. Spend your life seeing all of creation in these terms, remaining in the teaching of Jesus, and witness how your life is totally transformed.

Day 33

The Cross of Christ Restores . . . Obedience

And by this we may be sure that we know him, if we keep his commandments. He who says, "I know him," but disobeys his commandments is a liar, and the truth is not in him; but whoever keeps his word, in him truly love for God is perfected. By this we may be sure that we are in him: he who says he abides in him ought to walk in the same way in which he walked.

1 JOHN 2:3–6

Truly, truly, I say to you, if any one keeps my word, he will never see death.

JOHN 8:51

Some years ago I attended a religion class at a Catholic college that included several "spiritual talks." On one particular night the talk was on obedience. I must have heard this particular talk more than once; I remember it too well to have sat through it only once. It was as though everyone had received the same set of lecture notes on how to deliver this new teaching on obedience.

First the presenter would go up to the board and write "obedience." Then he would break the word apart: *ob* meaning "toward" and *oedire* meaning "to listen to." The presenter, who would always seem to have found in this exercise some moment of personal liberation, would then smile and say, "So you see, to obey is not some slavish exercise, but rather an exercise in listening to someone."

If one were to take a survey of all those educated in Catholic schools over the past forty years, I'll bet there would be any number of experiences similar to mine. Suddenly a vow of obedience to a religious superior meant only the obligation to listen to him or her before deciding whether to carry out a particular instruction. Lay people adopted similar attitudes toward the teaching of Christ and his Church.

Through such disobedience, the sin of Adam and Eve is committed all over again. I suppose it is no coincidence that I have had to attend more than a few seminars on improving one's listening skills. Here again, I know I'm not alone. A whole generation of us learned to parrot back phrases to show how well we listened, with unfortunate results. When you repeat the gist of the conversation back to the speaker, the vast majority reacts as though you are being condescending. Those in a slightly more charitable frame of mind assume that the subject of discussion is so boring that the only way you can stay awake is to repeat everything that is being said.

> *Obedience leads to acceptance into the kingdom; disobedience leads to expulsion from paradise.*

"Not See Death"?

When Jesus says, "If any one keeps my word," he is talking about obedience. When Jesus says about the Father, "I do know him and I keep his word" (John 8:55), we understand him to mean that he is doing what the Father sent him to do. Similarly, John equates obeying the commandments with keeping his word (see 1 John 2:5). It is pretty clear that the more traditional understanding of "listening" implies doing exactly what God tells us.

It is *this* kind of obedience that is Jesus' condition to not "seeing" death.

Disobedience was at the heart of the original sin. Have you ever watched a toddler assert his independence by resisting with every fiber of his little being the grown-up who wants him to do something he really, really doesn't want to do? Some have suggested that we are born princes but turn to frogs. It seems far more likely that we are born princes who would rather be frogs than members of a royal family. So, our fallen nature works overtime to redefine what it does not want to do in the first place.

"Keep His Word"

Jesus teaches us that we have to keep his word. Of course, this is the cross for many of us. We'd rather go our own way than follow the way of Jesus, but to go our own way is to face the horror of death without hope. When Jesus says that those who keep his word will never "see death," what does he mean?

I studied this passage for several hours. I found that this passage was translated differently in the Vulgate to include the word "forever," so that the intended meaning would be that the person would still die but not forever. Many commentators simply ignore it.

"Seeing death" is referred to in only one other place in the New Testament, in the Gospel of Luke, where Simeon had been told that he would not "see death" until he had seen the "Lord's Christ," or God's Messiah. Holding the infant Jesus in his arms, Simeon prayed, "Lord, now let thy servant depart in peace, according to they word; for mine eyes have seen salvation, which thou hast prepared in the presence of all peoples, a light for revelation to the Gentiles, and for the glory of thy people Israel" (Luke 2:29–32).

In the Scriptures, death was portrayed as an angel — and not necessarily a good angel. Remember, death entered the world because of sin, and resulted in separation from God. The angel of death passed over the Israelites to take the Egyptian firstborn when Pharaoh rejected God.

So, what was Jesus saying? The most satisfying commentaries interpret the words of Jesus to mean that those who are obedient to the will of God, as revealed through Jesus' teaching, will never see this angel of death; rather, when their earthly life ends, they will be greeted by the Lord and brought into eternal life. Obedience leads to acceptance into the kingdom; disobedience leads to expulsion from paradise.

The secret to obedience is given to us in John's Gospel, when Jesus teaches that he is the vine and we are the branches. Our life depends upon remaining part of him — which we do by being obedient to his commands and partaking in his Body and Blood offered in the Eucharist. John in his letter says that we can tell if we are "abiding" in Christ by our actions: Are they Christ-like?

The power to be like Christ, of course, comes from dying to ourselves and allowing Christ to live within us. This requires more than simply listening to or parroting the words of Christ; this requires a complete abandonment to him.

Every day the official prayer of the Church begins the same way, by praying Psalm 95: "Come, let us worship the Lord," echoes the refrain, inviting us to see our Savior, our Creator, the God to whom we belong. With the invitation comes a warning: "If today you hear his voice, harden not your hearts."

Steps to Take as You Follow Christ

Ask—Am I obedient to the commands of Jesus?

Seek—To be open to God. Receive the Eucharist and ask God to enrich you with his Body and Blood, enabling you to be an obedient son or daughter, abiding in Christ

Knock—Meditate on 1 John 2:3–6. How well do we know him? How much of our disobedience is due to our own ignorance of Christ? Are we disobedient children because we do not really believe that the Father loves us, and wants what is best for us?

Transform Your Life—Accept the transfusion of life that is the Eucharist, an exchange of our sin-tainted, mortal flesh for the immortality of the God-Man. Live the Eucharist realizing that Christ remains in you. When you are tempted, call upon the presence of Christ to empower you to be obedient.

Day 34

The Cross of Christ Restores . . .
The Dignity of Work

*And on the seventh day God finished his work which he had done.
. . . So God blessed the seventh day and hallowed it, because on
it God rested from all his work which he had done in creation.*

GENESIS 2:2–3

*"If I am not doing the works of my Father, then do not believe me;
but if I do them, even though you do not believe me, believe the
works, that you may know and understand that the Father is in
me and I am in the Father." Again they tried to arrest him, but
he escaped from their hands.*

JOHN 10:37–39

I spent five rather fruitless years teaching high-school theology.
Early on it was clear to me and to my students that this wasn't
what God wanted me to do. However, they weren't quite so
adept at figuring out their own vocations. When I asked a student what he wanted to do with his life, he would rattle off the
same tired list of professions as his classmates. They would do
whatever made the most money.

As I threw him out of class one day, one of my students yelled
as he headed to the principal's office, "Who needs this? Mr.
Steinbrenner is a good friend of my dad. He told me that he'd
give me a job."

Yes, he was talking about *that* Mr. Steinbrenner.

The saddest thing about my teaching experience was my inability to communicate to my students the fact that all the money in the world could not make them happy. I told them of the miserable rich people that I had known, who hated their work and counted the minutes to retirement. The world is full of human beings who suffer under the curse of Adam: "Cursed is the ground because of you; in toil you shall eat of it all the days of your life; thorns and thistles it shall bring forth to you; and you shall eat the plants of the field. In the sweat of your face you shall eat bread till you return to the ground, for out of it you were taken; you are dust, and to dust you shall return" (Genesis 3:17–19).

The cross of Christ redeems us and restores the dignity of work that God intended from the beginning when he created us. In John's Gospel, when Jesus refers to his words and miracles he has a simple name for them, "the works of the Father." Why do the healings of Jesus seem so miraculous to us? Because we live in a world where everything is degenerating — where "thorns and thistles" spring up, no matter how long we toil.

Jesus shows us a different path: effortless production, where "the barren has borne seven, but she who has many children is forlorn" (1 Samuel 2:5); where those who do not sow, reap nonetheless; and where the fishermen let down their nets, and at his word cannot contain their catch. This is the fruitful, fulfilling kingdom of God.

God's Purpose for You

The *Spiritual Exercises* of St. Ignatius of Loyola were developed from his own experiences. He was sure that being a knight would bring him happiness. However, his career as a knight was short-lived. Ignatius was felled by a cannonball and had to recuperate.

While recovering, Ignatius read the lives of the saints, and found that when he read these stories, he was left with a feeling of contentment. When he read other, more worldly works, he felt agitated. Ignatius concluded that when we are where God wants us to be, we are at peace no matter how much conflict we face.

Jesus is the perfect example of this. He did the work of God, even when his life was threatened. He knew nothing would happen to him until the appointed time, and so he moved about Israel with a deep sense of trust in God

What keeps us from experiencing the fruitfulness of the work that God has for us? Ignatius called these things "disordered attachments," referring to anything that rivals a part of us that is meant for God: money, sex, pleasure, or anything else. When people make decisions about their lives based solely on a disordered attachment, they can expect a ton of "thorns and thistles" in their lives. The beauty of the rose deceives until the thorns dig into flesh.

Who will we follow, Christ with his victorious cross or fallen humanity into its grave?

Ignatius often reflected on the state of the world and the effects of sin, as contrasted with the Incarnation, God becoming one of us and saving us from our plight. Who will we follow, Christ with his victorious cross or fallen humanity?

The first step to ridding ourselves of disordered attachments is to realize what those attachments might be. Whenever we have a tendency to rationalize that something is "holy," "untouchable," or "indispensable" — it is a pretty good indication that a disordered attachment is at the root. Only God is our holy and untouchable source of life. Giving anything else such a high priority is perpetuating a lie.

Next, we might look at our priorities in life. If you are reading this, it is evident that you care about your spiritual life. However, even spiritual people run the risk of making an ideology into a god. The people that Jesus argued with the most were spiritual people, especially those who considered themselves so good and holy that they did not recognize the God they claimed to serve, even when he appeared right in front of them. The Pharisees stand as a great witness that we must always be vigilant in searching for God, no matter how "spiritual" we become. God should be our priority; not our idea of who God is, but rather God as he really is.

St. Benedict spoke of the "opus Dei," the work of God that was the priority of the monk. In this context, he was referring to prayer. Prayer keeps us hooked into our Source of life. It should be more important to us than food or sleep — again because our very life depends upon it. Jesus came to redeem us, to overturn the curses that befell humanity because of original sin. By taking up our cross and following Christ even in our work, we can share in the "works of the Father" and be miracle workers in the eyes of the fallen world.

Steps to Take as You Follow Christ

Ask—Am I doing what God wants me to do?

Seek—To pray, to put God first in all things, in every aspect of your life. Ask God to bless your home and your work, making all that you do fruitful.

Knock—Meditate on Genesis 2:2–3. How do you rest from your work? How do you sanctify the Sabbath in your life? Do you trust enough in God's providence to take a day off? Spend some time reflecting on Jesus' Sabbath rest on Holy Saturday and what it could mean for you.

Transform Your Life—Allow the cross of Christ to restore the dignity of your work. This may not involve leaving behind your job, even if you took that job for the wrong reasons. God can transform anything into good. So what matters is what your motivation is in your work: are you building up the kingdom of God or are you trying to build your own kingdom?

The Power of the Cross

Day 35

The Cross of Christ Restores . . . Justice

I will surely gather all of you, O Jacob, I will gather the remnant of Israel; I will set them together like sheep in a fold, like a flock in its pasture, a noisy multitude of men. He who opens the breach will go up before them; they will break through and pass the gate, going out by it. Their king will pass on before them, the LORD at their head.

MICAH 2:12–13

But one of them, Caiaphas, who was high priest that year, said to them, "You know nothing at all; you do not understand that it is expedient for you that one man die for the people, and that the whole nation should not perish." He did not say this of his own accord, but being high priest that year he prophesied that Jesus should die for the nation, and not for the nation only, but to gather into one the children of God who are scattered abroad.

JOHN 11:49–52

Dr. Lena Allen Shore, a Polish Jew, survived the Holocaust by pretending to be Catholic. Catholic friends rescued her family on the very day they were to be sent away to a Nazi death camp, one of the most horrific examples of "scapegoating" in modern history. Her Catholic pretend name was Therese.

"Therese" and her brother were such model Catholics that, unaware of their guise, some Catholic friends called upon them to be godparents. They politely refused, unwilling to take their religious deception that far. Years later, Dr. Shore befriended a fellow Pole, Pope John Paul II. In his letters to Lena, the pope often tells his Jewish friend to "be herself," a poignant message to a woman who spent her youth pretending to be someone else.

Lena now dedicates her life to building bridges, emphasizing our common humanity under God. Having herself suffered the injustice of misplaced blame, Dr. Shore is a tireless advocate for contemporary "scapegoats." Hers is a powerful testimony to the inherent dignity of all people, even those most marginalized by society.

Desert Wanderer

In the Book of Leviticus, God outlines the duties of the high priest on the feast of Yom Kippur: "and Aaron shall lay both his hands upon the head of the live goat, and confess over him all the iniquities of the people of Israel, and all their transgressions, all their sins; and he shall put them upon the head of the goat, and send him away into the wilderness by the hand of a man who is in readiness" (Leviticus 16:21). In the Gospel of John, the high priest Caiaphas performs this same ritual guilt-laying, not on a scapegoat but upon the head of Our Lord Jesus Christ. The Gospel records that, after this council of the Sanhedrin, Jesus left and went into the wilderness (see John 11:54).

Although Caiaphas's pronouncement in this gospel reading was undoubtedly politically expedient, John tells us that the high priest was prophesying in his role as high priest, and not of his own accord. In other words, God turned Caiaphas's politically motivated pronouncement into a religious prophecy. Of course, from a political standpoint Caiaphas was dead wrong. The death of Jesus did not prevent the Romans from coming in and taking their "place": Both the Temple and the office of the high priest were soon destroyed by the Romans. Yet Jesus' death would lead to the gathering of the flock of God and would restore the relationship between humanity and the Father. In that sense, the death of this one man would save the people.

Jesus knew that people's desires were askew, and that the high priest was concerned for the Temple only as an edifice and his position only for its political clout. The ruins of human history are built on ill desire. Sadly, many of us who claim to be Christians bear a stronger resemblance to the high priest than to Christ. We desire not what is best for us but the forbidden fruit that looks pleasant to the eye.

As children, most of us couldn't wait to grow up; we longed to assume authority over ourselves. Jesus, on the other hand, always referred to himself as "son."

As children, most of us couldn't wait to grow up; we longed to assume authority over ourselves. Jesus, on the other hand, always referred to himself as a "son," and called his followers — including us — to be like children, to be like sheep, to be servants and followers of one Lord. In everything he did, the Lord maintained his core identity as the "Son."

From the cross, Jesus looked at the "disciple he loves," called him "son," and presented him to his new mother, Mary. (It is perhaps the greatest testament to Mary's exalted role in God's plan that she is considered not only the Mother of Jesus but of all the disciples he loves.)

Caiaphas and the prophet Micah both prophesied that Jesus would gather the children of God. Micah used the image of the gate being broken; Caiaphas proposed the death of the Lord as the way. How are we then to be drawn back into this filial relationship that the cross restores? By facing the cross with the disciple Jesus loved and our mother, Mary.

Like the Polish Catholics who saved Lena's family during World War II, we can never ignore the injustice or the scapegoats of society. Empowered by our relationship with God, we must stand up for those who are blamed unjustly for the sins of humanity. Jesus, the Scapegoat of God, has taken the sins of humanity into the desert; now true justice is tempered with mercy.

In standing up for justice, we must not become tyrants. Those who lead successful revolutions against injustice often become the next abusive regime. The cross of Christ teaches us a path of humility and obedience to God alone, not to any ideology but to Christ. Standing up for what is right is the duty of every child of God, and the Son of God has shown us the way. We strive to be like him, not to obtain some position or false power. The cross of Christ restores our status as children of God; like Our Lord we should ever remember that we are children of God and trust in Him alone.

Steps to Take as You Follow Christ

Ask—Do I see myself as a child of God?

Seek—Focus on the crucified Christ as you meet him throughout the day. Stand up for your brother or sister, always appealing to the brother or sister who might seek to harm him or her.

Knock— Meditate on Micah 2:12–13. Micah prophesies that the Lord will lead his sheep out of their captivity. In the violent journey of Christ out of the walled city of Jerusalem, we see a literal fulfillment of this prophecy. Are you one of the followers of Jesus on his way of the cross?

Transform Your Life—Realize that you are a child of God, reborn in Baptism when you shared in the death and resurrection of Jesus. Live out your Baptism, dying to yourself whenever you find yourself tempted to be a child of something other than the one true God.

Taking Up Our Cross . . .

(WEEK SIX)

As they went out, they came upon a man of Cyrene, Simon by name; this man they compelled to carry his cross.

MATTHEW 27:32

WE must sacrifice ourselves to God, each day and in everything we do, accepting all that happens to us for the sake of the Word, imitating his Passion by our sufferings, and honoring his blood by shedding our own. We must be ready to be crucified. If you are a Simon of Cyrene, take up your cross and follow Christ. If you are crucified beside him like one of the thieves, now, like the good thief, acknowledge your God. For your sake, and because of your sin, Christ was regarded as a sinner; for his sake, therefore we must cease to sin. Worship him who was hung on the cross because of you, even if you are hanging there yourself.

St. Gregory Nazianzen

Day 36

Taking Up Our Cross . . .
In Abandonment

Let us then cast off the works of darkness and put on the armor
of light; let us conduct ourselves becomingly as in the day, not in
reveling and drunkenness, not in debauchery and licentiousness,
not in quarreling and jealousy. But put on the Lord Jesus Christ,
and make no provision for the flesh, to gratify its desires.

ROMANS 13:12–14

"Go into the village opposite you, and immediately as you enter
it you will find a colt tied, on which no one ever sat; untie it and
bring it. If any one says to you 'Why are you doing this?' say, 'The
Lord has need of it and will send it back here immediately.'"

MARK 11:2–3

A young Israeli whose family immigrated to Brazil was studying
to be a rabbi. The rabbinical school happened to be near a Benedictine monastery, where one day the young man heard the
monks chanting the Hebrew psalms. Fascinated, he ventured
closer. Wanting to learn more about the men who prayed the
psalms so beautifully, one day the Jewish man introduced himself to one of the monks. As their conversation deepened, the
monk told the young man of Jesus, the Messiah.

Some months later, the student was in Rio de Janeiro when,
passing by a large Catholic church, he was drawn to step inside.
He walked in and made his way to the front of the sanctuary,

where there hung a larger-than-life crucifix. Standing in front of the cross, he said aloud to the crucified Christ, "Tell me if it is true. Are you the Messiah?"

When he told me the story and I asked him what happened, the young Catholic priest replied, "I'm here." His family had disowned him, but he remained strong in his belief and trust in Jesus, who had answered him from that cross.

Most of us who were raised in Catholic households may not appreciate the price of believing. We take it for granted. When I read the stories of converts, I am moved at the distance some will travel in order to come to Christ.

The early church fathers, always seeking the fuller sense of Scripture, thought that the colt "on which no one ever sat" represented the Gentiles who had not had the Word of God preached to them. By mounting the colt that the apostles brought to him, the fathers saw Jesus as symbolically inviting the Gentiles to take on his yoke. Abandoning ourselves to Christ requires something more than throwing off our cloaks and cutting palm branches. It involves "drinking from the chalice that he will drink and undergoing the baptism that he will undergo." This can lead to a radical redirection in our lives.

Going Wherever He Leads Us

In the case of my friend, abandoning himself to Christ involved the rejection of his family — as Christ had prophesied would happen to those who followed him (see Mark 13:12–13). For many of us this won't be the case. However, when we truly open our hearts to the cross of Christ and plead, "Tell me if it is true. Are you the Messiah?" we can be sure he will answer us.

I recently worked with fourteen women converts to put together a book, *The Catholic Mystique,* in which each recounted her entrance into the Catholic Church from other

Christian traditions. Each story entailed Christ pulling them along the path he had chosen for them. What is remarkable about their stories is the abandonment to Christ they share in common. Some of the women were ordained priests or ministers in the churches they had left in order to become Catholic. Many had left behind families and friends, just as my Jewish friend had done. The person who is truly abandoned to Christ, goes where the Lord calls him or her to go — even if it is "where they would not go."

> ✝ They were crying to be saved by God and his Christ. Ironically, a few days later they cried out, "Crucify him," bringing about that very act of salvation.

In a recent interview, British journalist John Bishop asked Father Benedict Groeschel about his future plans for the thriving community of the Franciscan Friars of the Renewal, which Father Benedict had co-founded. Father kept insisting that he had no plans except to be led. When Bishop pressed him, the friar answered all the more insistently, "No plans, just be led."

No one knows what the future holds. Abandoning oneself to the cross of Christ, one does not try to impose "my will" against "God's will"; rather, one prays daily, "God's will be done."

Lord, Save Us!

When the Lord entered Jerusalem on Palm Sunday, he was greeted as the Messiah. On Good Friday, the same crowd offered him up as the sacrificial lamb. We tend to interpret this as the crowd turning on Jesus, and indeed from a worldly perspective that is what seems to have taken place. We can relate to this fickle response. But if we look at what happened to Jesus, we'll see God's mysterious plan being enacted.

"Hosanna!" the people cried as Jesus entered the city. This is one of the few words in Scripture that is not translated into English (like *Alleluia; Amen;* and *talitha, koum*). How does "Hosanna" translate into English? In most English translations of Psalm 118:25, this word is translated "Save us!" It seems that it may have been this psalm that the people of Jerusalem were proclaiming as Jesus entered the city: "Save us, we beseech thee, O LORD! O LORD, we beseech thee, give us success! Blessed be he who enters in the name of the LORD! We bless you from the house of the LORD. The LORD is God, and he has given us light. Bind the festal procession with branches, up to the horns of the altar!" (Psalm 118:25–27). They were crying out to be saved by God and his Christ.

Ironically, a few days later they cried out, "Crucify him," bringing about that very act of salvation. At times we lose sight of how this mirrors the actions of their ancestors, the patriarchs of the original twelve tribes, who sold one of their brothers into slavery — and God used that act of treachery for his own end. Thus at the end of Genesis we hear Joseph proclaim, "As for you, you meant evil against me; but God meant it for good, to bring it about that many people should be kept alive, as they are today"(Genesis 50:20).

St. Paul tells us that we are to "cast off the works of darkness and put on the armor of light" — we are to conduct ourselves as people of light. Too often people try to escape or reject their cross; they flee to the darkness, escape in alcohol or sex, or immerse themselves in anger, all because things have not gone their way. Without the grace of God, this is our fate as well. Yet when we are handed a cross, if we abandon ourselves and trust in God as Christ did, what seems like defeat is in fact a victory! The evil that is done to us, God can mold into good. Then we can sing Hosanna to God in the highest, because the light of God will live in us and we will see everything in his light.

Steps to Take as You Follow Christ

Ask—Do I believe in God's providential care?

Seek—Cry out to God to save you. Realize what it means to say that God is your Savior. Frequently call to mind all that you need to be saved from and have recourse to God who alone can save you.

Knock—Meditate on Romans 13:12–14. Paul uses the image of armor that we wear, either of darkness or light. Much of what he terms the deeds of darkness are acts that typically happen at nightfall or in the secret of one's heart—they are acts that take place when we hide them from God and others. Reflect on how putting on armor of light and bringing all of your cares before God will change the way you see them.

Transform Your Life—Believe and trust in Jesus at all times. Do not allow the enemy to have a foothold into your life. Make *"Hosanna, save us, Lord"* the prayer that is constantly on your lips.

Day 37

Taking Up Our Cross . . .
In Reverence

Therefore let us be grateful for receiving a kingdom that cannot be shaken, and thus let us offer to God acceptable worship, with reverence and awe; for our God is a consuming fire.

HEBREWS 12:28–29

Jesus said, "Let her alone, let her keep it for the day of my burial. The poor you always have with you, but you do not always have me."

JOHN 12: 7–8

My three-year-old son has a tendency to be unruly at Mass. He seems to enjoy the power he can exercise over us in a crowded church. On one of his recent outbursts I took him to the back of the enormous cathedral, where, moments later, I felt for the first time that the Holy Spirit might have prompted his behavior. Had he not been acting up and had I not brought him to the back of the church, I would not have encountered two powerful images.

First I noticed the bishop, clad in red vestments, his hands extended in the *orans* position. It was the image of Christ on the cross. Now, I have been attending Mass all of my life and I know that the priest represents Christ, but I had never seen this as clearly as I saw it at that moment. There was something about the vestments and the outstretched arms that said to me, "This is Christ!"

A little farther back, I noticed something else: a young woman prostrate in the aisle of the church, her forehead touching the floor in adoration. To be honest, my first reaction was one of protest. I've been educated in Church circles, and know all about "correct" posture and behavior during Mass. I am also well acquainted with the "Judas game" some well-educated Catholics play at Mass, in which individual acts of worship are criticized for form rather than praised for intent. Instead of worshipping Jesus like Mary of Bethany, who reverently poured out expensive nard upon the Lord's feet and dried them with her hair; they resemble Judas, who chastised Mary for not selling the ointment and giving the proceeds to the poor.

As I continued to watch the young woman's prayerful prostration in the cathedral that day, it struck me that what the young woman was doing — whatever her motivation — was beautiful. In a certain sense, it was even prophetic, for it drew me back to what I was doing. In my heart I thanked her for her witness. Both the bishop and the woman in prayer made it possible for me to participate as fully as possible in the Mass that day, holding my son and offering myself with Christ to the Father in my own poor way.

Reverence and Worship

In *Earthen Vessels*, Benedictine Father Gabriel Bunge explains that the early church fathers recommended prostration — kneeling with the forehead to the ground — to overcome dryness in prayer. When the body expresses the humility and submission of true worship, the mind is better able to be in tune with God.

I witnessed this again last year, while visiting a community of priests, brothers, and nuns called the Community of St. John. This community is attempting to revive this ancient practice. Attending Mass at their monastery in rural Illinois, members of the community all prostrate themselves during the consecration of the Eucharist and again after receiving communion. It was without a doubt one of the most moving liturgies I have ever attended: Simple but reverent, in the presence of other people who were caught up in the consuming fire of God.

> *Reverence for Jesus should be our instinctive response to his presence, whether in the Eucharist or in another human being. Those who claim to follow Christ, yet lose sight of both his message and his person, fall prey to worshipping an ideology rather than a Divine Person.*

We live in a strange time. Differences are elevated on one hand and tolerance of these differences is seen as virtuous. Yet this toleration does not often extend to those who wish to worship God, especially in the liturgy. I thought of this again while I was dining as a guest of another monastic community. During the meal, several monks knelt out for some community infractions. There was nothing in their non-unified act that made the dinner less communal. If anything, it made it more real — symbolic of the various roles we all play in community at one time. If we cannot let the smallest infraction or deviation pass — the casual attire of the younger crowd, the Cheerios and sippy cups of the toddlers, or those who come in late or leave early — we cannot worship God very well.

Reverence for Jesus should be our instinctive response to his presence, whether in the Eucharist or in another human being. Those who claim to follow Christ, yet lose sight of both his message and his person, fall prey to worshipping an ideology rather than a Divine Person. If we are consumed with self, the consuming fire of God cannot touch us.

The Real Prayer of St. Francis

St. Francis of Assisi taught his followers to reverence Christ and his cross wherever they might find themselves. The prayer attributed to St. Francis that begins, "Lord, make me a channel of your peace," was in fact not composed by St. Francis; it was misapplied to him in a prayer book. The true prayer of St. Francis was one he taught his friars to pray whenever they would pass a Church or the sign of the cross made by two branches in a tree. They were to prostrate themselves toward the church or the cross and pray, "We adore you Christ and we praise you present here and in all the Churches throughout the world, because by your holy cross you have redeemed the world."

The cross reminds us of the true Christ, the one in the Gospels who was constantly misjudged by the religious figures of his day. If we are not careful, he will be misjudged by us as well. We need to worship him alone.

Steps to Take as You Follow Christ

Ask—Do I reverence God?

Seek—Find a way to adore God today, be it in the Eucharist or in the secrecy of your room, or anywhere. When you see the shape of the cross, say the prayer that St. Francis instructed his brothers and sisters to say, "We adore you O Christ. . ."

Knock—Meditate on Hebrews 12:28–29. What does it mean to offer acceptable worship to God? How is the kingdom we are offered by Christ unshakeable?

Transform Your Life—Make you life one of reverence toward God at all times. Let your focus be on remaining in God's presence, rather than judging and criticizing those around you.

Day 38

Taking Up Our Cross . . .
To Follow the Lord

Humble yourselves therefore under the mighty hand of God, that in due time he may exalt you. Cast all your anxieties on him, for he cares about you. Be sober, be watchful. Your adversary the devil prowls around like a roaring lion, seeking some one to devour. Resist him, firm in your faith, knowing that the same experience of suffering is required of your brotherhood throughout the world.

1 PETER 5:6–9

Simon Peter said to him, "Lord, where are you going?" Jesus answered, "Where I am going you cannot follow me now; but you shall follow afterward." Peter said to him, "Lord, why cannot I follow you now? I will lay down my life for you." Jesus answered, "Will you lay down your life for me? Truly, truly, I say to you, the cock will not crow, till you have denied me three times."

JOHN 13:36–38

Father Benedict Groeschel spent a month on life support after a car struck him at a busy intersection in Orlando, Florida. He has no memory of that month but his fellow religious have shared with him the outpouring of prayers and sacrifices on his behalf during that time of uncertainty.

Father Benedict was in Florida that weekend because he was scheduled to speak to 125 priests at a workshop the following Monday; instead he was confined to a hospital bed. Monsignor Andrew Cusack, who was in charge of that workshop, stood at the podium in Father Benedict's place and prayed for the friar's recovery. A month later, Father Benedict emerged from the hospital. At almost the same time, Monsignor Cusack was laid to rest. He had died suddenly upon his return to New Jersey. None of us knows what the future holds.

> No matter how pure our motives may seem, until we trust in him more than we trust in ourselves, we are doomed to fail. If we are truly to follow Jesus, we must unite ourselves with him and trust him totally.

"Where Are You Going?"

When St. Peter heard that Jesus was going somewhere, he wanted to follow the Lord. Jesus refused, and told the apostle that he would follow later. Peter protested: He was willing to lay down his life for Jesus (again something that he ultimately would do later). Then Jesus dropped a bombshell: That very night, Peter would deny him three times.

The final battle to following Jesus is the battle of self. No matter how pure our motives may seem, until we trust in God more than we trust in ourselves, we are doomed to fail. To truly follow Jesus, we must unite ourselves with him and trust him totally.

The story of Peter's ultimate sacrifice in Rome has long been told. When Nero's persecution of the Christians broke out in Rome, Peter fled. On his way out of the city, he met Jesus on the Appian Way. Shocked to see the Lord, Peter asked, *"Domine, quo vadis?"* ("Lord, where are you going?")

Jesus looked at Peter and said, "I am going to Rome, to be crucified again." Hearing the words of the Lord, Peter turned back to Rome to face his own death. He was crucified upside down, declaring himself unworthy to die the same way as the Lord he had denied. "You cannot follow me now, but you shall follow afterward," Jesus had told Peter. And he did, when the time was right.

The Greeks had two words for time, *chronos* for chronological time (clock and calendar time) and *kairos* for the "right" or "opportune" time. Jesus often made the distinction to his disciples, who thought more in terms of chronological time than of God's time. When Peter first declared his intent to the Lord, it was not yet time; the *kairos* moment — God's time — did not come until Peter had witnessed to the truth of the gospel in Rome.

When the Jews celebrate Passover, the celebration begins with a question: "Why is this night different?" In this way they enter into God's time — when God intervened, did something to change the very course of history. On the night before he died, Jesus took bread and wine and declared it his body and blood. "Do this in memory of me." Once again it was *kairos* time, God's time, just as it is every time we interrupt the daily grind of chronological time to enter God's time in the Mass.

Everything happens when God wants it to happen. Following Christ is a matter of surrendering to God's time, of leaving behind our own plans in order to be led by Christ. Our goals and plans are always secondary to what God intends for us.

In a letter, Peter told the followers of Christ to be humble, and God would exalt them. No doubt he was thinking of all the times he had been humbled by Jesus' superior knowledge of him. In time, Peter grew wiser, and came to understand that the only stance of the follower of Christ is "Lord, depart from me for I am a sinful man." For it is only then that he will hear the Lord say, "Follow me."

"Be watchful," Peter also tells us. The path is difficult, and our opponent seeks to overtake and devour us like a roaring lion. This is not a journey for the timid or the proud, but a journey for the humble. There is much to fear ahead, but we know of someone who can be trusted to lead us "through the valley of evil."

"Cast all your anxieties on him, for he cares for you," Peter admonishes us. Like Peter, may we learn to listen when the Lord tells us to "let go and to cast your net on the other side." No matter what perils face us, the Lord will always tell us the way to go.

Steps to Take as You Follow Christ

Ask—How often do I trust my own instincts, and how often do I entrust myself to Jesus?

Seek—Try to live each day with a resignation to God's will, accepting each moment with the expectation that God might be breaking through to you.

Knock—Meditate on 1 Peter 5:6–9. Think about the experiences of Peter in the Gospels and the Acts of the Apostles and the words that he writes here. What lesson do they convey? How might the devil be seeking to devour you in your attempts to follow Christ?

Transform Your Life—Make an amendment to live humbly. Cast all of your hopes and anxieties on the Lord. Realize that following Jesus means living a life of trust not in your way but in God's way, the way of the cross.

Day 39

Taking Up Our Cross . . .
Be Prepared

Whoever, therefore, eats the bread or drinks the cup of the Lord in an unworthy manner will be guilty of profaning the body and blood of the Lord. Let a man examine himself, and so eat of the bread and drink of the cup. For any one who eats and drinks without discerning the body eats and drinks judgment upon himself. That is why many of you are weak and ill, and some have died.

1 CORINTHIANS 11:27–30

Now on the first day of Unleavened Bread the disciples came to Jesus, saying, "Where will you have us prepare for you to eat the passover?" He said, "Go into the city to a certain one, and say to him, 'The Teacher says, My time is at hand; I will keep the passover at your house with my disciples.'" And the disciples did as Jesus had directed them, and they prepared the passover.

MATTHEW 26:17–19

While I was preparing material for the National Catholic Educators Association convention in St. Louis a year ago, my son came into the room and turned on the stereo. Out boomed the voice of Archbishop Fulton J. Sheen. It was a tape that had remained in the stereo from the time I had been listening to some of the archbishop's talks as I compiled a book of Eucharistic meditations based on his writings. The book was later published as *Praying in the Presence of Our Lord with Fulton J. Sheen.*

The archbishop read from Paul's First Letter to the Corinthians: "For any one who eats and drinks without discerning the body eats and drinks judgment upon himself. That is why many of you are feeble and sick, and a number have died" (1 Corinthians 11:30, NEB). The archbishop read it very dramatically, and commented that it was interesting no one ever took that verse into account. Then, without any further remark, he went on to talk about something else.

That night I found myself thinking about the passage, over and over. I knew from previous courses that the meaning of the passage confused many commentators. The next morning, I did a quick study and found that the Greek word that Paul used for "died," *koimaō* literally means "fallen asleep." Thought it often means "death," it can also mean actual sleep.

> We who are called to the Lord's Supper have a duty to prepare ourselves for our encounter with the Lord. We must examine ourselves so that we may worthily take up his cross, from the moment we sign ourselves with holy water from the baptismal font. In the Eucharist, our sacrifice is joined to the one sacrifice of Christ at the moment of kairos, God's "opportune time."

We know from the Acts of the Apostles that St. Paul once preached a very long sermon, which caused a boy, Eutychus, to fall into such a deep sleep that he toppled out a window. Most of the worshippers presumed he was dead. Paul momentarily interrupted his preaching to check on Eutychus and declare him alive. Paul then went on with the breaking of the bread, in what we would call today the rest of the Mass.

It dawned on me that Eutychus might have been the inspiration for what Paul was writing to the Corinthians when he referred to "some who have even fallen asleep"!

Know What You Celebrate

How often do we attend the Sacrifice of the Mass without really knowing why we are there, or without paying attention to what is going on? This is how we eat and drink without discerning: We grow sick of the Mass, and don't get anything out of it. We grow feeble in our faith or — like poor Eutychus — we are bored to death!

In "The Constitution on the Sacred Liturgy," the fathers of the Second Vatican Council noted that pastors have a duty to ensure that the "faithful take part fully aware of what they are doing, actively engaged in the rite and enriched by its effects" (SC 11). Unfortunately, when it comes to the Sacrifice of the Mass, those who should know are often as muddled as those who look to them for the answers.

On the day of the Last Supper, when he instituted the Eucharist, Our Lord sent his apostles ahead to make the preparations. They were to tell the "certain one" that his "time was at hand." The fact that no name is given is interesting. Some commentators have noted that it could be that the Matthew did not want to reveal the name of the individual, to protect them from the authorities; of course, this makes sense only if the Gospel were written much earlier than is commonly believed. Another possibility is that the generic "certain one" is you and I; in much the same way as the "disciple whom Jesus loved" can be the reader or hearer of the word as well as the historical individual.

In the Book of Revelation Our Lord says, "Behold, I stand at the door and knock; if any one hears my voice and opens the door, I will come in to him and eat with him, and he with me"

(Revelation 3:20). We who are called to the Lord's Supper have a duty to prepare ourselves for this encounter with the Lord. We must examine ourselves so that we may worthily take up the cross he gives us. In the Eucharist, our sacrifice is joined to the one sacrifice of Christ, it is our entrance into his *kairos*, "God's time."

Being Prepared

What will we say when the messengers of Our Lord come to us and tell us that the time is at hand, and the Lord wishes for us to prepare for his Passover? Will we open the door of our hearts and welcome him?

Maria Montessori, founder of the Montessori method of learning, wrote a book in the early twentieth century about the Mass for Children. She began by describing the inside of a church: candles lit, altar cloths set on the altar. Something very special must be about to take place here, she said. Just as the disciples prepared for the Passover, the Last Supper of the Lord, so we must prepare to welcome the Savior before we approach his banquet.

Being prepared for Mass is essential to the disciple and follower of Jesus Christ who wishes to be enriched with his teaching and be fed with his Body and Blood. St. Paul's admonition to examine ourselves is paramount if we are not to eat and drink judgment upon ourselves — but rather partake in the Way, the Truth, and the Life.

Steps to Take as You Follow Christ

Ask—How well do I prepare for the Eucharist I receive at Mass?

Seek— Try to participate fully in the Eucharist each time you are present; if possible, attend daily. Be mindful of what you do at

Mass, what you hear and how you respond. Learn more about the Mass.

Knock—Meditate on 1 Corinthians 11:27–30. What does St. Paul mean when he says that those who do not discern bring judgment upon themselves? What can you do to examine yourself before participating in Mass to avoid doing it absent-mindedly?

Transform Your Life—Know what you celebrate when you are at Mass; mean what you do with every gesture and prayer, and especially when you receive Holy Communion.

Day 40

Taking Up Our Cross . . .
In Imitation of Christ

Have this mind among yourselves, which is yours in Christ Jesus, who, though he was in the form of God, did not count equality with God a thing to be grasped, but emptied himself, taking the form of a servant, being born in the likeness of men. And being found in human form he humbled himself and became obedient unto death, even death on a cross.

PHILIPPIANS 2:5–8

When he had washed their feet, and taken his garments, and resumed his place, he said to them, "Do you know what I have done to you? You call me Teacher and Lord; and you are right, for so I am. If I then, your Lord and Teacher, have washed your feet, you also ought to wash one another's feet. For I have given you an example, that you also should do as I have done to you."

JOHN 13:12–15

Verily always seemed to materialize whenever I needed a piece of furniture for my office space. It was as though some alarm went off, and he would come running up to ask how he might help. I once asked him where his name came from, and he said the Bible. When I looked at him quizzically, he quoted the verse with great pride, "Jesus said: 'Verily, Verily I say unto thee.'"

At Verily's retirement, I was struck with his humility, standing proudly in a suit and tie as those in charge gave speeches about how much his janitorial expertise would be missed. Every day this man performed the most mundane tasks with great dignity, from setting up a Christmas crèche for the company or bringing flowers in from his garden to set up by the tabernacle in the chapel. The motivating force in his life was Christ, and his vocation — like all followers of Christ — was to imitate the example that Jesus had given his apostles.

✝ *Jesus has given us an example of service to follow. It may seem a little too commonplace for most of us who, like St. Peter, prefer to proclaim the greater things we can do — such as laying down our lives for him. And like the apostle, we are apt to fail miserably, even deny that we know the Lord. Perhaps we should start — and even finish — with less lofty goals, for God's ways are not our ways.*

Some of the greatest saints spent more time sweeping the church than preaching in it. When St. Francis of Assisi heard from the cross of Christ to rebuild the Church that was falling into ruin, he began to clean up the rubble of the church where the vision had occurred. This became a lifelong habit; whenever he traveled, he always brought along a broom to clean churches. The Legend of Perugia records that St. Francis "suffered a great deal, in fact, when he entered a church and saw it dirty." I have seen St. Francis with a bird on his shoulder, holding the Scriptures or even a cross. I have never seen him holding a broom but, according to this tradition, this was the wooden "cross" he always carried with him.

I have already mentioned Blessed Teresa of Calcutta, who also would pick up a broom and sweep the streets upon arriving at one of her many communities spread throughout the world.

The Power of the Cross

You and I might wonder why such holy people would take up such menial tasks when all were seeking an audience with them — and we would be just like the Apostle Peter who, when Christ began to wash his feet, refused him.

Humble Yourself

We are all so much like St. Peter. If you have ever been asked to have your feet washed on Holy Thursday, I'll bet your first reaction was to turn down the offer with modern variations of Peter's protestations. Jesus called Peter "Satan" (right after he called him "Rock") and declared, "You are not thinking the thoughts of God, but the thoughts of men" (Matthew 16:23), all because Peter rejected Jesus' announcement of the suffering and death that he would endure in Jerusalem.

In the language of John's Gospel, the washing of the feet becomes a symbolic acting out of the Incarnation of Jesus. Once again Jesus lowers himself, taking the form of a slave by performing a servant's task; after he finishes the work he has been given to do he rises, taking back his garment of divinity and resuming "his place" at the right hand of God. This time he also tells his followers that he has given them an example to follow: They are not to exalt themselves but to humble themselves and serve the rest. One of the most ancient titles for the pope, as a successor of St. Peter, is "Servant of the Servants of God." The saints all share in common this ability to be the servant of the servants, whether they are poor materially or spiritually.

I have been a Catholic since I was baptized, three weeks after my birth. In forty-five years I have met people of every rank and class within the Church, and I have found that often the holiest people are also the most hidden. They are the men and women who are often found cleaning up the church on Monday mornings or Saturday afternoons, often praying the rosary as they go about their tasks. If you are looking for evidence that the miraculous gifts are still at work in the Church today, you are most likely to find these gifts among such "hidden saints." Two of the greatest religious figures of the past century in North America — Blessed André Bessette and Venerable Solanus Casey — both functioned as porters, a fancy name for the house servant who answers the door.

Doing Great Things

When we think of doing great things for Christ, we need to be careful that it is not Satan's suggestion. Jesus has given us an example of service to follow. It may seem a little too commonplace for most of us, who, like St. Peter, prefer to proclaim the greater things we can do — such as laying down our lives for him. And like the apostle, we are apt to fail miserably, even deny that we know the Lord. Perhaps we should start — and even finish — with less lofty goals, for God's ways are not our ways.

The cross of Christ reveals the love God has for us; to follow Jesus is to imitate his example, to do as he has done for us to others. Sometimes that means offering a glass of water to a little one. Sometimes it means picking up a broom and sweeping a dirty hallway. Sometimes it means taking note of someone that others are passing by. These are small things in the eyes of the world, but the actions of great saints in God's kingdom.

Having the mind of Christ and accepting his cross means turning away from the tree of temptation, where Satan is enticing us to eat so that we might be like God, and turning toward the tree of the cross, where we find what being like God is really like. Jesus told his disciples that the pagans liked to lord it over each other but it wasn't to be that way with them. Two thousand years later, have we learned that lesson? Whose feet are we washing, beside our own?

Steps to Take as You Follow Christ

Ask—Am I willing to do small things for Christ?

Seek—Volunteer to do a task that no one wants to do, a menial or unpleasant one, all the while uniting yourself with the Passion and death of Jesus.

Knock—Meditate on Philippians 2:5–8. Paul says that we should have the mind of Christ, and Jesus told Peter that he was thinking like men and not God. How is having the mind of Christ different than the thoughts that we are apt to naturally have about life issues? Do your thoughts clash with the gospel message? Are you trying to be like the god you imagine, or the God Jesus revealed by his cross?

Transform Your Life—Seek to follow the example of Christ in all that you do. Be solicitous for the care of others. Learn the truth that in dying to self you are born into eternal life.

Day 41

Taking Up Our Cross . . .
To Stay with Jesus

If one member suffers, all suffer together; if one member is honored, all rejoice together. Now you are the body of Christ and individually members of it.

1 CORINTHIANS 12:26–27

But standing by the cross of Jesus were his mother, and his mother's sister, Mary the wife of Clopas, and Mary Magdalene. When Jesus saw his mother, and the disciple whom he loved standing near, he said to his mother, "Woman, behold, your son!" Then he said to the disciple, "Behold, your mother!"

JOHN 19:25–27

Serving as an altar boy for the Stations of the Cross on Friday nights in my parish church is one of my favorite boyhood memories. The priest would be dressed in a black cassock, with a lace surplice and a purple stole. Two servers carried candles but the lucky one got to carry the cross. The cross bearer didn't have to genuflect and kneel twenty-eight times, as everyone else did; in an ironic twist, the one who carried the cross had it easier than the rest. Being the cross bearer was such a coveted position that often the priest had to devise a way to award the honor to one of the three of us. All of this implanted within me that in life, "The lucky one gets to carry the cross."

Our parish used the stations of St. Alphonsus Ligouri, which began at each station, "We adore thee, O Christ, and we praise thee, because by thy holy cross thou has redeemed the world." Over and over again those words would be repeated as a mantra that planted itself deeply within. Christ was to be praised above all things because by his suffering he had redeemed the world.

The meditations of St. Alphonsus were a simple recalling of the Passion of Jesus, but added something else. After the priest recalled the particular event of the Passion associated with each station, we would read the response, accusing ourselves of treating Jesus as the crowd on Good Friday had those many years ago. We had done this by the way we treated others and the way we treated the great gift of God's love in our own lives.

Failure and suffering are a part of every life; seen through the Passion of Christ, they can be a part of God's plan for us.

As we walked from one station to the next we sang the *Stabat Mater*, literally the "Sorrowful Mother," as though we were accompanying the Blessed Virgin Mary as much as Jesus on this journey to the cross. We would sing: "At the cross her station keeping, stood the mournful mother weeping, close to Jesus to the last."

When I was lucky enough to hold the cross, I felt more united with Christ than the crowd, more aligned with Mary as I stood at the foot of the cross. It would take me years to understand that being united with Christ meant being united with the sinners in the crowd, not separate from them. He forgave them and me.

Those evenings always ended with Benediction of the Blessed Sacrament, to remind us that the Christ who had suffered, died, and rose again remained with us now in the "breaking of the bread." Our adoration of him made up for our sinful rejection of him in the past. Through the hymns and incense we praised and adored Christ, thanking him for the gift of repentance. Walking out of the church on those Friday nights, the world never seemed quite the same.

The Way of the World

Sometimes after the stations I would join my classmates at a function of the public school we attended. They would ask me where I had been. "Church," I would tell them. They would look at me in unbelief. In my young and very fertile imagination, I thought of them as the angry crowd surrounding Jesus during his Passion. Why should my being at church cause them such discomfort?

But it did.

I realize now that the simple devotion that I participated in throughout my youth taught me a lesson that my friends did not receive: Failure and suffering are a part of every life. Seen through the Passion of Christ, they can be a part of God's plan for us.

When I look back over the years, I realize that my life has not gone according to my youthful plans. No one's does. In my class, a number of people were unable to handle their unexpected disappointments. Several turned to alcohol and drugs. One even took her own life. What a tragedy! In my youthful pride, I neglected to share with my classmates what I had learned at church; my light remained hidden under a basket. Now I am sometimes haunted by a dream, in which I am once again serving at Stations of the Cross. Now my school friends are there too, holding the cross next to me. How lucky they are, I think. Yet sadly, it is only a dream.

The Way of the Cross

In these meditations we have reached the summit of Calvary. We see Our Lord nailed to the tree of the cross. That tree is a vine, and we are called to be the branches — all of us. We can unite ourselves with Christ and live in him — accepting Mary as our Mother, too — or we can stand separated from him, doing our own individual thing.

I once read a personal essay written about attending Mass where the writer advised the reader to get to church early to find a pew where you will likely have no one sitting anywhere near you to distract you. I confess there have been times that I have felt this way too, but I can see how sinful such a view is — how "separation" even in the name of God is not of God.

Jesus came to reunify all those separations brought about by original sin—whether they be nationality, gender, or language. "For by one Spirit we were all baptized into one body — Jews or Greeks, slaves or free — and all were made to drink of one Spirit" (1 Corinthians 12:13). Our sinful self rebels against this notion; we want to judge others rather than forgive in Christ. This is our cross! If we hold it in front of us, we will have a constant reminder of the One who died for the sins of the world — to save "them" and "us."

Steps to Take as You Follow Christ

Ask—Do I feel "lucky" to carry the cross that God has given me?

Seek—Keep the cross of Christ before you at all times. Let it be a reminder of Christ's forgiveness for you when you feel sorrowful for your sins. Let it be a sign of God's love for others when you are tempted to judge. Let it be a light that you can share with those whose lives you touch.

Knock—Meditate on 1 Corinthians 12:26–27. Do you think of yourself as a part of Christ's body? What changes are necessary for you to make in order to act as a member of the body of Christ rather than as an individual follower of Jesus?

Transform Your Life—Realize the difference that embracing the cross of Christ makes in your life. Learn to see the world in a new way and to see what Jesus meant when he said, "Behold, I make all things new" (Revelation 21:5).

Day 42

Taking Up Our Cross . . .
Be Not Afraid

There is no fear in love, but perfect love casts out fear. For fear has to do with punishment, and he who fears is not perfected in love. We love, because he first loved us.

1 JOHN 4:18–19

There was a great earthquake; for an angel of the Lord descended from heaven and came and rolled back the stone, and sat upon it. His appearance was like lightning, and his raiment white as snow. And for fear of him the guards trembled and became like dead men. But the angel said to the women, "Do not be afraid; for I know you seek Jesus who was crucified. He is not here; for he has risen, as he said. Come, see the place where he lay."

MATTHEW 28:2–6

"There are no accidents," insisted Father Benedict Groeschel as he began to recover from the injuries he suffered in Florida. This strong statement of faith is similar to what Jesus told the disciples on the road to Emmaus: "O foolish men, and slow of heart to believe all that the prophets have spoken! Was it not necessary that the Christ should suffer these things and enter into his glory?" (Luke 24:25–26) Not an accident. . . necessary!

Father Groeschel frequently quotes St. Augustine in this regard: "God does not cause evil, but that evil should not become the worst." So, when a car struck him that January night, Father

Benedict's faith told him that there was a reason for this cross, a reason that ultimately God would reveal in time. This is the power of the cross for the follower of Christ: No matter what happens to us or can happen to us, we are not defeated.

Years ago I worked with someone who told me that her mother had labeled her and her brother as "accidents" — two unwanted, unpleasant surprises. Unwilling to think that a parent would say such a thing, I assumed my colleague's recollection of her mother's words was exaggerated.

This is the power of the cross for the follower of Christ, no matter what happens to us or can happen to us we are not defeated.

Some years later, I was introduced to her mother. In the course of conversation, the topic of abortion was raised. The woman pointed at her daughter and said, "If abortion had been legalized when I was young, I would never have had any children!" By that time she was an old woman; her daughter, who was divorced, lived with her and was a faithful companion. I pointed out that, had abortion been legalized, she would now be alone. "Wouldn't that be great!" the mother replied.

I left their home feeling very sad for both of them. Without the gospel message, some people see only accidents in their lives — all of which have prevented them from reaching some dreamed of earthly paradise. They never seem to realize they cannot reach this paradise without help from above.

Reactions

Coming to the tomb of Jesus that first Easter morning, the women discovered an angel there, the rock rolled away. It was a shocking and unexpected sight. The guards, who were there to make sure that the disciples did not steal the body of the Lord, were also witnesses to this. They were overcome with fear — to the point of being "like dead men."

One experience, two groups of people, two different reactions. One group looks at the empty tomb and rushes to tell what they have witnessed. The other group is paralyzed by the life event. This wasn't just something that happened thousands of years ago; it happens every moment of every day. Those who see the cross as the end of their life, meet death there; those who believe and place their trust in God, find in the cross life and victory.

St. Peter Chrysologus (the "golden-worded") was known for his clear and simple style of preaching. About the angel's appearance at the tomb, he preached, "Pray that the angel would descend now and roll away all the hardness of our hearts and open up our closed senses and declare to our minds that Christ has risen, for just as the heart in which Christ lives and reigns is heaven, so also in the heart in which Christ remains dead and buried is a grave."

For those who do not believe, life unfolds as a series of accidents. When a follower of Christ sees his life in exactly the same way, Jesus calls that person foolish, slow to believe. Someone like that needs to redirect his attention to the cross.

Gifts

The procession of the cross that begins and ends each celebration of the Eucharist should help us to redefine our lives whenever we witness it. As the Mass begins we join all of our crosses to the cross of Christ, asking the Lord to have mercy upon us for our inability to see. We listen to the Scriptures to once again learn about all the necessary events of our lives, proclaim the Church's belief as our own, and give thanks to God as we offer the sacrifice that he has provided for us. We then receive the Living God before the cross leads us back into the world!

Having received the life of Christ in us, we are better able to extend that love to others. I was reminded of this again a few years ago, when I met another family who also had an unplanned child. In the presence of the child they said what a gift they had been given — like nothing they could have ever dreamed of asking for, an incredible blessing. Their joy mirrored that of God the Father, who could not contain himself in heaven when his Son walked the earth. He opened up the heavens to exclaim, "This is my beloved Son, with whom I am well pleased" (Matthew 3:17).

That same Son would experience horrible suffering at the hands of cruel men. Assured of the love of the Father, he knew that ultimately the Father would not let him down. When you and I are finally convinced in the same way that God loves us, we will welcome whatever comes our way in this life and see it with a vision that others will marvel at. On that day we will say, "Alleluia. Praised be God!"

Steps to Take as You Follow Christ

Ask—Is life a series of "gifts" from God or tragedies?

Seek—Encounter the empty tombs of life with the expectation that they are signs of the Risen Christ.

Knock—Meditate on 1 John 4:18–19. How do you view the events of your life, as God punishing you or as God showering you with gifts? Is your image of what God is like from the way Jesus reveals God to us or from some other source?

Transform Your Life—Accept the cross whenever it presents itself to you in daily life. Do not flee from it. Do not shrink from it, but embrace it in the name of Jesus. Learn from it, be enlightened by it, find in it the key to living a fruitful life. Think of this every time that you sign yourself with the cross.

Appendixes

"The cross is the key to understand the Gospel, seeing how each one of its passages is as an introduction to understand that mystery."

Archbishop Bruno Forte

Appendix I

Questions for Group Discussions

See www.osv.com/powercross for a online version of this study guide.

The Cross of Christ Teaches Us . . . (Week One)

Day 1. Our Mission

+ Reflecting on the temptations of Christ, see if you can find other ways that his true mission was hidden in the lies of Satan.

+ Have you had an experience where you were prevented from committing an evil act because of some outside interruption to your plans?

Day 2. To Live the Gospel

+ What steps can you take in order to notice Christ more in those the world considers the "least"?

+ Are there people in your own family whom you neglect, who fit into the categories of Matthew 25?

Day 3. How to Pray

+ When has your prayer been most heartfelt?

+ Are there times when your prayer has been one of desperation?

Day 4. About Repentance

+ Have you experienced a radical Christian conversion in your life?

+ Share a remarkable story of faith that you have personally witnessed.

Day 5. *How to Trust and Give Thanks*

+ Are there times you have experienced remarkable answers to prayers you have prayed to God?
+ Do you trust that God will give you the things you need?

Day 6. *Reconciliation*

+ How does forgiving someone free you from bondage?
+ Who are those who are most unloved in the world today?

Day 7. *How to Love*

+ What keeps you from loving everyone on the face of the earth?
+ What are some ways that we can die to ourselves and live for others?

The Cross of Christ Unites . . . (Week Two)

Day 8. *The Temporal and Eternal*

+ How can living for Christ bring light to those who live in darkness?
+ Name some areas of darkness in the world that have yet to be touched by the light of Christ

Day 9. *Those Divided by Sin*

+ Who are the people that you feel most separated from, and how can you reach out to them with the mercy of God?
+ How does the cross of Christ bring about the unity lost by original sin?

Day 10. In Humility

+ How does humility help the body of Christ to function together as one?
+ When is humility not a virtue?

Day 11. In Liberty

+ How free are you really?
+ What "gods" or "masters" are you serving throughout the day?

Day 12. Those Who Suffer for Justice

+ Look at the life of someone who has lost his or her life trying to help another. What can you learn from that person's life?
+ What can you do to relieve the suffering of others?

Day 13. Us in the Work We Have to Do

+ Can you think of people who seem to be perfectly placed where God wants them to be?
+ What is the role of friends and family in helping us to know what God's will for us is? How does the story of Joseph in Genesis bring this home?

Day 14. God's Mercy and Love

+ How does judging others make you feel?
+ What would it be like not to pass judgment on yourself?

The Cross of Christ Transforms . . . (Week Three)

Day 15. How We Worship

+ Do you worship God "in spirit and truth"?
  What do you need to surrender to God?

Day 16. How We See Jesus

+ Does making Jesus "our friend" make him too small?
+ Do we see Jesus as the all-powerful God, able to work powerfully through our weakness?

Day 17. How We Forgive

+ What do Catholics mean when they speak of Purgatory? (See the Catechism of the Catholic Church #1030–32)
+ How do indulgence practices speed up the action of God's grace in a person's life? (See the Catechism of the Catholic Church #1470–79)

Day 18. Law and Love

+ How do you view God the Father's role in the crucifixion of Jesus?
+ Who do you need to show charity (love) to the most?

Day 19. Our Lives

+ How much is your faith affected by the empty promises of advertisements?
+ Share an example of God's faithfulness in your life.

Day 20. Our Priorities

+ Where does sacrificial love fit into your life?
+ Is there a benefit to you in loving sacrificially?

Day 21. How We See Ourselves

+ What do you mean when you say, "Lord, have mercy"?
+ How does being "in Christ" manifest itself in your life?

The Cross of Christ Illumines . . . (Week Four)

Day 22. Blindness

+ What does the account of those whose physical blindness is cured teach us about the spiritual path?
+ Is there "darkness" that you prefer to the light of Christ?

Day 23. Lag Time

+ How do you handle periods of waiting on God's response to your prayers?
+ How are God's ways different from your way of doing things?

Day 24. Weakness

+ How do you view weakness in yourself, as a blessing or a curse?
+ How does the world view weakness?

Day 25. Death

+ How do nonbelievers in Christ face death?
+ How do you remember those who have died?

Day 26. Our Choices

+ How do you see the City of God and the City of Man present in the world today?
+ How would you describe your lifelong pilgrimage toward God?

Day 27. The Truth

+ How can we know Jesus, and as a result know God better?
+ What parts of the movie *The Passion of the Christ* are from Scripture? Where is the rest from?

Day 28. The Way to True Unity

+ What can you do to bring about unity with other followers of Christ?
+ Why is division wrong?

The Cross of Christ Restores . . . (Week Five)

Day 29. Life

+ What can you learn from the different ways Jesus responds to Martha and Mary?
+ How does the loosing and binding power that Jesus gives to his Apostles continue to be exercised by the Church today?

Day 30. Forgiveness

+ How might the movement of Jesus—bending to the ground and then rising to speak to the crowd—symbolize his cross and resurrection?
+ How is sin destructive?

Day 31. The Image of God

+ Do you listen more to the message of your culture or of the gospel?
+ How would looking at a serpent on a pole heal someone from a poisonous snake bite?

Day 32. Our Freedom

+ What is it that makes you feel incomplete?
+ What concrete steps do you need to take to change your behavior?

Day 33. Obedience

+ What does it mean to be obedient to God?

+ What keeps you from being obedient?

Day 34. The Dignity of Work

+ Do you feel God is calling you to do something special in your life?
+ How can you help others to see God's purpose for them?

Day 35. Justice

+ What is your relationship with Mary, the Mother of Jesus?
+ How does your status as a child of God affect your relationship with other people?

Taking Up Our Cross . . . (Week Six)

Day 36. In Abandonment

+ How does God use the evil that people do to bring about good?
+ How does believing in God's providence help you to let go of judgments about the present moment?

Day 37. In Reverence

+ What can you do to increase your reverence toward God?
+ How reverent are the people in your church?

Day 38. To Follow the Lord

+ How are God's ways different than your ways?
+ How can recognizing your sinfulness and admitting it help you to be more open to Christ?

Day 39. Be Prepared

+ How can you learn more about the Mass?
+ Are you prepared to welcome Christ?

Day 40. In Imitation of Christ

+ Who is the holiest person you have ever known?
+ What did this person do that exhibited his or her sanctity?

Day 41. To Stay with Jesus

+ Have you ever been called upon to be a modern Simon of Cyrene—to help another carry his or her cross?
+ How can you spread the message of the power of Christ's cross?

Day 42. Be Not Afraid

+ How have you experienced the power of the cross in your life?
+ How do the eyes of faith help you to see beyond what others see?

The Power of the Cross (Preliminary Lenten Days)

Ash Wednesday. Eternal Life or Death?

+ How would you react if you saw two monks pull into your driveway today bringing the coffin that would one day contain your dead body?
+ Are you motivated by a fear of death or by a love of eternal life?

Thursday after Ash Wednesday. Jesus' Invitation

+ How do you view the Passion of Jesus? Do you see the willing suffering of the Son of God as a sign of God's love for you?
+ Is the crucifix displayed prominently in your place of worship? In your home? Where you work?

Friday after Ash Wednesday. How Much We Need Jesus

✝ What purpose does the spiritual practice of fasting serve in your Christian life?

✝ At what other times, besides the hour fast before the reception of Holy Communion, does the Church ask her members to fast?

Saturday after Ash Wednesday. A Matter of Life and Death

✝ What are the results of original sin in the lives of fallen humanity? (See the Catechism of the Catholic Church #400)

✝ How do you bury your dead?

Appendix II

How to Use This Book as a Lenten Devotional

The book can be used at any time of the year, but those who wish to use this book as a Lenten devotional should begin here. These "preliminary" reflections will take you from Ash Wednesday through the following Saturday. The next day, the First Sunday of Lent, start at the beginning of this book. "Week One" will correspond to the First Week of Lent.

There are forty days in Lent, beginning on the First Sunday of Lent and ending on Holy Thursday. The evening Mass of the Lord's Supper on Holy Thursday signals the beginning of the Easter Triduum. The main body of this book follows those forty days and takes the reader to Holy Saturday.

The Power of the Cross

The first man was from the earth, a man of dust; the second man is from heaven. As was the man of dust, so are those who are of the dust; and as is the man of heaven, so are those who are of heaven. Just as we have borne the image of the man of dust, we shall also bear the image of the man of heaven.

1 CORINTHIANS 15:47–49

HOW precious the gift of the cross, how splendid to contemplate! In the cross there is no mingling of good and evil, as in the tree of paradise: it is wholly beautiful to behold and good to taste. The fruit of this tree is not death but life, not darkness but light. This tree does not cast us out of paradise, but opens the way for our return.

This was the tree on which Christ, like a king on a chariot, destroyed the devil, the Lord of death, and freed the human race from his tyranny. This was the tree upon which the Lord, like a brave warrior wounded in his hands, feet and side, healed the wounds of sin that the evil serpent had inflicted on our nature. A tree once caused our death, but now a tree brings life. Once deceived by a tree, we have now repelled the cunning serpent by a tree. What an astonishing transformation! That death should become life, that decay should become immortality, that shame should become glory!

Theodore the Studite

Ash Wednesday

ETERNAL LIFE OR DEATH?

"You are dust, and to dust you shall return."

GENESIS 3:19

"And when you fast, do not look dismal like the hypocrites, for they disfigure their faces that their fasting may be seen by men. Truly, I say to you, they have their reward. But when you fast, anoint your head and wash your face, that your fasting may not be seen by men but by your Father who is in secret; and your Father who sees in secret will reward you."

MATTHEW 6:16–18

Virginia Cyr loved to visit the beautiful monastery of Saint Meinrad's Archabbey in southern Indiana. On one such visit she witnessed the funeral service of a monk, whose body, in a simple pine box, lay in state in the Archabbey church. During the funeral Mass, the pounding of hammers echoed as the pine lid was fixed in place and the box nailed shut. The monks then carried their confrere to the monastic cemetery and buried him there.

It was at that moment that Virginia decided that she, too, wanted to be buried in a simple pine coffin when she died. She mentioned this to the monk who accompanied her to the cemetery. He promised that the monks would fulfill her wish.

Born with cerebral palsy, Virginia's short life was one filled with bodily pain. Yet this remarkable woman was full of joy. I became acquainted with Virginia through her diaries, which she had entrusted to the care of a Benedictine monk at Saint Meinrad. In 2004 I helped to have them published in book form under the title of *Virginia Cyr: God's Little Hobo*.

A friend of Virginia's recounts that when the monks finished her coffin, two of them drove the four hours to Kokomo, Indiana, where she lived to show her their handiwork, hoping it would meet her approval. Virginia welcomed them and praised their workmanship as she viewed what would be the final resting place for her body. She kissed the wood as though she were venerating the cross of Christ on Good Friday. Then she asked the monks to place her in it so that she could make sure that it was a good fit.

The monks helped her out of her wheelchair and gently placed her in the pine box, straightening out her gnarled limbs. As she lay in the box, she thanked them profusely for their act of charity. Virginia's joyful reverence of the wood of her coffin can be explained only by her faith in the Passion, death, and resurrection of Jesus. She could embrace the cross in her life because she believed in life beyond this earthly existence.

Remember You Are Dust

When I was taking graduate courses in theology, one of the first requirements was a course entitled "Theological Anthropology," a rather complicated name for the study of the human person and nature as revealed by God. In other words, who does God say we really are?

I remember only one thing from that course, something that the professor repeated in his thick Irish brogue a number of times throughout the semester: "Every year on Ash Wednesday, when a priest puts ashes on your forehead and says, 'Remember man that you are dust and unto dust you shall return,' it is heresy!"

My first reaction to this was probably the same reaction that you are having reading it — "What?" It took me awhile to understand what he meant. In the Book of Genesis, when God tells Adam, "You are dust, and to dust you shall return," God is saying to Adam and to all of his descendants that if we choose to disobey and reject His will (i.e., to sin), then death is our end. However, as my professor was pointing out, those who believe in Christ have been freed from original sin by the Passion, death, and resurrection of Christ. Death is no longer to be our final end.

So why does the Church do this ritual every Ash Wednesday at the beginning of Lent? Because it reminds every Christian that, without Christ, we are as good as dead! The ashes, symbolizing repentance, form a cross on our foreheads, so that we "remember" who we are without Jesus — and with Him!

> ✝ Archbishop Fulton Sheen remarked that there are two types of people in the world; those who are living to die and those who are dying to live.

Living in a Post-Christian World

Ours is a post-Christian world, where Christians exist but Christianity has ceased to be the governing force in society. Consequently, many Christian beliefs continue to be accepted by people who have long forgotten that these beliefs are connected entirely to belief in Jesus Christ. People speak of going to heaven and living after death as though such a thing were possible apart from belief in Christ. Yet this is not what science or experience teaches any of us — rather, this is what God has promised to those who place their trust in him.

Without Christ we are dust and to dust we shall return! Doesn't life bear this out?

Archbishop Fulton Sheen once remarked that there are two types of people in the world: those who are living to die, and those who are dying to live. The first group follows the Epicurean philosophy: "Eat, drink, and be merry, for tomorrow we die." They spend their lives fighting against the inevitable natural decline that is this earthly life; they try to maintain a youthful appearance and to experience pleasure as often as possible (usually at the expense of others). Any hardship is viewed as unbearable. Anything unplanned is terminated. They sacrifice their unborn children, their marriages, their vocations, all for some Utopia on earth that does not exist. The only reality they believe in, the only god they worship, is death.

The second group follows Christ their Savior. They die to many impulses that are motivated by such a false final reality; to them, the present moment is not for squeezing in as much pleasure as possible. They believe that they shall live forever in Christ, and that whatever suffering the present moment brings is nothing in comparison to the glory that awaits them with Christ. They realize, as Venerable Solanus Casey once said, "Life here in the exile is so short and uncertain, that it seems to me it ought to have another name." By joyfully embracing the will of God, they find themselves in the paradise the other group only dreams about.

Someone who truly embraces the cross experiences this glory in a way that confounds those who witness it. It is for this reason that Virginia Cyr exhibited great joy in the midst of her horrible suffering. At any given moment, our ability to trust Christ and to endure joyfully the cross we have been given will determine the glory we experience here and now.

Two Ways to Pray

Jesus spoke about two types of prayer: the prayer of the hypocrite (the "actor"), and the prayer done in secret. Do we live our lives focused on what others will see or on what God sees? Which concerns us more, whether another human being approves of us, or God's approval?

Actors are not themselves, and are unable to live out the purpose for which they were created: ultimately, God's purpose. If you are an actor, at some point you will come to the realization that your life is a sham, a fake, that you have betrayed your calling in life. Ironically, when Jesus first addressed the problem of hypocrisy, he was speaking to the "religious" people of his day! Religion is no guarantee of being the way God wants us to be. How we pray and how we view the cross in our life, on the other hand, is an indication of what road we are traversing—the way of the cross or the way that leads to eternal damnation. Remember, you are dust, but "if any one is in Christ, he is a new creation; the old has passed away, behold, the new has come" (2 Corinthians 5:17).

Steps to Take as You Follow Christ

Ask—Am I living my life in fear of death or in anticipation of eternal life in Christ?

Seek— Try to focus on Christ as the motivation for all of your actions throughout the day. Be conscious of whom you are trying to please in all that you do.

Knock— Meditate on Genesis 3:19. How does Baptism wash away original sin? What is the purpose of recalling that without Christ we are all living to die? How does the cross of Christ defeat death?

Transform Your Life—Make the cross of Christ your banner of hope. See in the victory of Jesus' cross a life-changing invitation to overcome all the evil forces that try to keep you from being who God has created you to be and to drive you away from your true purpose in life.

The Power of the Cross

Thursday After Ash Wednesday

JESUS' INVITATION

For many, of whom I have often told you and now tell you even with tears, live as enemies of the cross of Christ. Their end is destruction, their god is the belly, and they glory in their shame, with minds set on earthly things. But our commonwealth is in heaven, and from it we await a Savior, the Lord Jesus Christ, who will change our lowly body to be like his glorious body, by the power which enables him even to subject all things to himself.

PHILIPPIANS 3:18–21

"If any man would come after me, let him deny himself and take up his cross daily and follow me. For whoever would save his life will lose it; and whoever loses his life for my sake, he will save it. For what does it profit a man if he gains the whole world and loses or forfeits himself."

LUKE 9:23–25

In the old horror films, one often sees the image of someone holding out a cross and something else (a vampire, werewolf, or devil) recoiling in horror, cowering, and usually fleeing in the opposite direction. In the battle between good and evil, the victory of the cross was always assured. Not the physical object, of course, so much as what the cross symbolized: the victory of Jesus Christ over the forces of evil, worked out in his Passion and death on the cross.

In recent years I have noticed a new trend in horror films: In the battle against evil, someone pulls out a cross or crucifix at the appropriate time — but now the symbol of Christ merely enrages the evil force, which knocks the cross out of the hands of the good person before unleashing its full rage, destroying him or her.

Why this change?

In the 1960s, the effectiveness of those who carried the cross in the civil rights movement in the United States was the subject of the nightly news. Some were lynched, and were shown hanging from trees; others were shot dead. Yet in the end the gospel of Christ was heard, and the price of taking up the cross with its risk was clearly portrayed in the lives of those martyred for that cause.

A Christian Church without the cross is akin to Flannery O'Connor's "the church of Christ" without Christ.

As our nation grew in affluence and influence, carrying the cross seemed beneath many of us. People began to rationalize about the nature of evil, reasoning that perhaps not everything is as black and white as it was in the past. Suddenly the one holding the cross was perceived to be a fraud, in some cases more evil than the force he or she was battling.

Today if a screenwriter were to depict a confrontation of the cross in the style of the classic horror films, it is likely that those who would recoil from the cross would not be those associated with evil, but rather those once thought to be defenders and believers in the power of the cross.

Add to all of this the message of "toleration over truth" that has been the focus of organized religions in the past forty years. Some have claimed that the cross was offensive, that it "alienated" people, causing Christian schools and hospitals to take the crosses off the walls of their rooms, so as not to offend non-Christians. In churches, crosses were replaced with images of the resurrected

Christ, as Christians proclaimed themselves to be "an Easter people" (as though the cross did not convey the image of resurrection).

Fear of the Cross

Forty years ago, civil rights leaders — many of them Christian ministers — endured great suffering because they believed in God's ultimate victory. Today those who once would have used the cross to defeat evil now are apt to fear this powerful symbol of the Christian faith. How do we explain this modern fear of the cross? How has the symbol of salvation become such a threat to those who should embrace it?

Fear of the cross is now a recognized psychological disorder called staurophobia, coming from the Greek word, "*stauros*" for cross and "*phobia*" for fear. Overcoming this fear involves clarifying what one associates with the cross. What does the sight of the cross trigger within an individual?

Jesus said that if anyone would follow him they had to deny themselves and take up their cross. A Christian church without the cross is akin to Flannery O'Connor's "the church of Christ" without Christ. Unfortunately these voices are heard too often in churches today: Those who don't want to think about the price of sin, who have a difficult time with much of the gospel message, who redefine humility to look a lot like pride, who spend a lot of time talking about "my rights" rather than God's righteous judgment and holy will. Paul calls them "enemies of the cross."

What We Should Fear

Before the movie *The Passion of the Christ* was released, angry groups were speaking out against it. Some claimed it was too violent — and indeed, the Passion and death of Our Lord was too violent! Executions are gruesome affairs. However, facing the horror of what Jesus endured in his crucifixion helps us to overcome our own aversion to the crosses we have been given to carry: It shifts our focus back upon what Our Lord did as a sign of God's great love for us. After the release of Gibson's movie, a news report broke about a Catholic college in New York that had replaced the crucifixes upon the walls of its classrooms over spring break — crosses that had been taken down some twenty years previously!

Orthodox Christians prepare for the season of Lent each year by listening to the story of Zacchaeus the tax collector. The Gospel of Luke tells us that Zacchaeus was "short in stature," so Zacchaeus climbed up a tree. (For the Christian, this immediately reminds us of the cross; in a sense, Zacchaeus mounted his cross so that he could *see* Jesus.) Jesus bid Zacchaeus to come down "from that tree" so that he might stay at the tax collector's house. Zacchaeus eagerly welcomed Jesus, repented of his sin, and promised to make restitution. Salvation had come to him!

The early Christians saw the cross everywhere in the Scriptures. They sought to configure their lives to the crucified Christ. They did it in the way they prayed, whether praying with arms extended, or "breaking the bread" of the Lord's Body, or drinking from the chalice that he had accepted from the Father.

The cross is the sign of our salvation. May we rediscover the power of that sign and embrace it as the weapon he has bequeathed to us. May we hold that sign of our salvation out against all the evil powers that threaten us with an undying faith, and in his name experience the power of his saving death!

Steps to Take as You Follow Christ

Ask—Do I fear the cross of Christ or do I embrace it?

Seek— Place a crucifix in a prominent place in your home. Look upon this sign of our salvation upon rising and before you retire for the night, asking Christ to help you to "take up your cross" and follow him.

Knock—Meditate on Philippians 3:18–21. What are you living for? Do you see the saving power of the cross or are you an enemy of the cross? Do you believe in the power of Christ?

Transform Your Life— Believe in the gospel and experience the liberating effects of taking up your cross and following Jesus. Make your life one that will not be spent looking backward in regret for all the good that you did not do—focus on the good that you can do right now!

Friday after Ash Wednesday

HOW MUCH WE NEED JESUS

The Spirit and the Bride say, "Come." And let him who hears say, "Come."...He who testifies to these things says, "Surely I am coming soon." Amen. Come, Lord Jesus!

REVELATION 22:17, 20

Jesus said to them, "Can the wedding guests mourn as long as the bridegroom is with them? The days will come, when the bridegroom is taken away from them, and then they will fast."

MATTHEW 9:15

Older Catholics may remember a time when they would fast from midnight until they went to Mass. At Mass they would finally break their fast with a divine "breakfast," receiving Christ in the Eucharist. This practice meant that the celebration of the Eucharist was almost always held early in the morning, or if held later usually meant that almost no one received the Eucharist, since the fast would be too severe.

In 1964 Pope Paul VI changed the required fast to one hour before Mass. Since that time, due to poor religious instruction, the practice of fasting has suffered quite a bit. At a Mass that I attended in Anaheim, California, the young people seated directly in front of me were eating popcorn moments before Mass began. Being a lifelong sinner who judges people way too much, I waited to see if they would still go to Communion. They did—and I'm sure they felt no compunction in doing so.

Regarding fasting before receiving Eucharist, Father Alexander Schmemann says that from the earliest moments of the Christian Church's history, "it had been understood as a state of *preparation* and expectation — the state of spiritual concentration on what is about to come. Physical hunger corresponds here to spiritual expectation of fulfillment, the 'opening up' of the entire human being to the approaching joy."[5]

The pre-Communion fast is something the individual does that joins him or her to the Church that is always in the state of "fast," awaiting the coming of the Lord. Our fast ends when the Lord calls us to himself. He is the Bread come down from heaven. He is the Living Water that will quench our thirst. He is the Way, the Truth, and the Life!

> ✝ Fasting can be the same as dieting but the motive is not to lose bodily weight but to lose the worldly concerns that weigh on us, to lighten our minds and hearts so that we can truly lift them up to the Lord.

Schmemann explains: "In the early church this total fast had a name taken from the military vocabulary; it was called *statio,* which meant a garrison in the state of alarm and mobilization. The Church keeps 'watch' — she expects the Bridegroom and waits for Him in readiness and joy."[6]

Spiritual Health

We need to recapture the spiritual practice of fasting in order to remember how much we need Jesus. The type of fasting that most of us are familiar with is the type advocated by our doctor, not our Father. The doctor is apt to warn us that we are killing ourselves with the amount of food we eat, while our Father has sent his Son to feed us with the Bread of Life — a food that sadly we often are not hungry enough to eat with full knowledge of the eternal benefit that is being offered to us. A young child feeding upon candy gathered at Halloween, from the Christmas stocking, or from an Easter basket has no appetite for a nourishing dinner — so, too, many of us no longer are truly starving to be fed by Christ.

I have struggled with weight as an adult, something that was absolutely not a problem when I was younger and very thin. What I have noticed about my own eating habits is that I often eat not because I am hungry but as a distraction. As I have pulled away from this habit, like a reformed alcoholic notices how much everyone drinks, I have taken notice of how much we all overeat. Archbishop Sheen once remarked that what we in the United States consider "fasting" would be "feasting" in many parts of the world!

Fasting can be the same as dieting, except that the motive is not to lose bodily weight but to lose the worldly concerns that weigh on us, to lighten our minds and hearts so that we can truly lift them up to the Lord. When we decide not to bury our problems by eating more food or turning up the volume on our MP3 player, radio, or television, we are left with our need, and then with a question. Can anyone save us?

You Deserve a Break

One of the resurrection appearances of Jesus to the apostles has Jesus grilling fish and bread on the shore of the Sea of Galilee. It is a very human image of the Son of God, one with which we can all readily identify. The apostles had been fishing all night long, and had caught nothing. No doubt they were tired and they were hungry. Jesus directs them to cast their net to the "other side" and they will find some fish. They obey him and so many fish fill the net that they are unable to pull it into the boat. "Come and have breakfast," Jesus calls to them (John 21:12), inviting them to take a break and enjoy the meal he has prepared for them.

We live in an age of nonstop advertisements. They assault us in everything that we see on the city street, hear on the airwaves, pop up on the Internet. They all promise to save us from some unsightly end, and while some may deliver us and offer some relief, all of them can do so for only a short time. It is the Bridegroom, Jesus, who can truly save us and that is why fasting is so necessarily a part of the Christian life; without it we lose sight of the fact that the real thing that we hunger and thirst for is not a thing at all, it is not some fruit hanging from a tree that is "a delight to the eyes," (Genesis 3:6), but rather the Son of God offering us salvation from the tree of the cross.

A favorite prayer of the early church was *Maranatha*, "Come, Lord." It is a beautiful prayer, centered and focused on asking the Lord to come to us in whatever the present moment brings and begging him to return as he promised. This is the prayer of every Eucharist, when we invite Jesus to transform the gifts we bring into his Real Presence. It is the prayer at every Baptism; the catechumen is immersed in the waters to die to self and to live for Christ. It is the prayer that we raise when the cross of the present moment threatens to crush us under its severe weight.

The Holy Spirit and the Bride — that is, the Church — cry out, "Come!"

Steps to Take as You Follow Christ

Ask—How greatly do I feel the need for Christ in my life?

Seek— Practice fasting before your reception of the Eucharist. Also find special times to fast before high points in the Christian year and during high points in your own life so that you may always remain focused on your need for Christ. Try doing more than is required by the Church.

Knock— Meditate on Revelation 22:17, 20. What did Jesus say about two or more gathering in his name? Who are you waiting for?

Transform Your Life— Foster and keep before you the need that you have for Jesus. Make your constant prayer to Jesus one of entreating him to come, to be present, inviting him to be a part of your life.

Saturday after Ash Wednesday

A MATTER OF LIFE AND DEATH

But he laid his right hand upon me, saying, "Fear not, I am the first and the last, and the living one; I died, and behold I am alive for evermore, and I have the keys of Death and Hades."

REVELATION 1:17–18

The Pharisees and their scribes murmured against his disciples, saying, "Why do you eat and drink with tax collectors and sinners?" And Jesus answered them, "Those who are well have no need of a physician, but those who are sick; I have not come to call the righteous, but sinners to repentance."

LUKE 5:30–32

Once I was visiting Holy Spirit Monastery in Georgia with a friend. When we arrived, one of the monks informed us that evening prayer would be a little delayed because one of the monks had died and they were awaiting the arrival of his body. My friend's face turned white. Never in her forty-plus years had she ever been in the presence of a dead body.

I found this amazing, having witnessed funerals from the time I was five or six years old, when bodies of the deceased were often "waked" in their own homes. Yet her parents had not wanted her to witness death as a child, and she had not bothered to confront it as an adult.

So we sat toward the back of the Abbey Church with the other non-monks in attendance. The monks were gathered at the door, awaiting the arrival of the body of their brother monk. It was placed on a flat surface (no coffin) and brought forward a few feet, with the help of several feeble monks, who stopped a few inches from where we stood.

The pallor of the lifeless shell spoke of the finality of death. I had seen it many times before. I had even been blessed to be with several people at the moment of death, hearing their last breath escape, watching their eyes go up, giving me an understanding of why the ancients believed that the soul came into the body through the soft spot of a baby's head and left through the same portal.

In some ways, the moment of death is something like a whimper. It is seldom the drawn-out affair an actor portrays, exaggerated to communicate the tragedy of what is unfolding. While birth may take hours, death often needs only the hundredth of a second.

A culture that keeps death at a distance doesn't hear the gospel message very clearly. If we forget or try to ignore the final end that awaits us without Christ we are like the terminally ill patient who thinks that if he or she avoids a visit to the doctor, his or her condition won't worsen.

Some monks bury the dead by dumping the body into a grave and throwing some lime over the corpse to aid in the decaying process. The Benedictines I have known use a simple pine box. Both end their funeral rites by individually throwing dirt onto either the corpse or the coffin — thereby fulfilling this counsel of their founder, St. Benedict, to bury the dead.

Out of Sight

This experience gave me two vivid images about how we approach death: My friend, who for over forty years had never witnessed a dead body in person; and the monks, who simply threw some dirt on the remains of their deceased brother.

My friend is symbolic of those who seek to keep death at a distance. When someone dies, we cremate the body and scatter the ashes the same way past generations might have emptied an ashtray. We don't want to think about it; we want to avoid any mention of it. Yet we constantly portray death in movies and music. We avoid burying the dead, and as a result are endlessly haunted by them.

Monks are not haunted by the dead. Neither do they forget them. They see in the brother who has passed from this life a reminder of their own mortality; the deceased leaves behind the shell of his body, just as they one day will leave theirs. This reminds them of their purpose, and of how short the opportunity they have to fulfill this purpose. In life as in death, ultimately all that matters is God!

A culture that keeps death at a distance doesn't hear the gospel message very clearly. If we forget or try to ignore the final end that awaits us without Christ, we are like the terminally ill patient who thinks that by avoiding a visit to the doctor, his or her condition won't worsen. Yet we know that it will only grow worse without help.

Following Jesus is a matter of life and death. Jesus claimed that he could save us from death, and in order to change the way we think—to have a true *metanoia* "changing of the mind" — we need to know what it is that Our Lord is rescuing us from. Facing death, whether that of family or friends, helps us to face our own death head-on.

At the recent funeral of a young man, his grieving mother arose and appealed to the man's friends to see in her son's death a call to conversion. Her message to her son's friends is relevant to all of us: now is the time to answer the call of Jesus to repent!

The Cure

When Jesus was questioned about the kind of people with whom he associated, he told the Pharisees that it was the sick who needed a doctor. We all are the "sick," fatally wounded by original sin. We do not get along with each other in the way that God intended, we tend to see differences rather than see each other as brothers and sisters. We tend to overpower others rather than humble ourselves by taking the way of the cross that Jesus laid out as the road to redemption.

Death is the final separation, the final consequence of original sin. However, there are other effects we carry throughout our lives if we do not submit to Jesus. When Adam and Eve fell they immediately realized they were naked — different from one another. Then God put enmity between nature and humanity, increased the woman's birth pangs, made her subservient to the man, increased the burden of the man's work, which now would produce thorns and thistles . . . all of this the result of original sin.

Jesus came to save us from all of this. This is why we are not to judge. This is why Paul could be bitten by the serpent and live. This is why husbands are to be as "Christ" to their wives, who "took the form of a slave." This is why in Christ there is neither Greek nor Jew, East or West!

In the Book of Revelation, when Our Lord appears to St. John, he says, "I died, and behold I am alive for evermore, and I have the keys of Death and Hades." In his life, we who believe (place our full trust in) in him also have the possibility of life, and this has to change the way we exist in this world, both now and at the hour of our death.

It is the realization that in Christ I am going to live forever; therefore I take up my cross and learn my daily lesson from him.

Steps to Take as You Follow Christ

Ask—How does viewing Jesus as my savior from death help me to face head-on the deaths of loved ones and even my own death?

Seek— Fast from passing judgment on anyone today. Realize in this little dying to yourself you are opening yourself to see others as God sees them.

Knock— Meditate on Revelation 1:17–18. Imagine Jesus touching you with his right hand and lifting you up from your death. What other areas of your life are dominated by death rather than the life of Christ? Ask Our Lord to free you from all death.

Transform Your Life— Do not shy away from death. Attend the funerals of loved ones and use the experience to engage your faith in Christ. Pray for others, ask the saints to pray for you, seeing in them living examples of the promise of Christ to save us from death.

Notes

¹ Virginia Cyr, *Virginia Cyr: God's Little Hobo* (Indiana: Our Sunday Visitor, 2004), 56–57.

² Pope John Paul II, General Audience, October 13, 1999, 3–4.

³ I once told someone who was fairly jaded that I was praying a novena to St. Thérèse for her, and I also told her about the roses. On the ninth day of the novena, her husband showed up at the door with several dozen roses.

⁴ Alexander Schmemann, *The Eucharist* (Crestwood, N.Y.: St. Vladimir's Seminary Press, 1980), 210. Thankfully this book is back in print and available from St. Vladimir's Seminary Press.

⁵ Father Alexander Schmemann, *Great Lent* (New York: St. Vladimir's Seminary Press, 2003), 49.

⁶ Schmemann, 50.

Praying the Rosary: With the Joyful, Luminous, Sorrowful, and Glorious Mysteries

Rediscover ... Deepen ... Contemplate ...

Based on the format suggested by Pope John Paul II in his apostolic letter *Rosarium Virginis Mariae* ("The Rosary of the Virgin Mary"), authors Michael Dubruiel and Amy Welborn help you:

Rediscover — or experience for the first time — the comfort, hope, and strength so many have found in this ancient prayer.

Deepen your love of Christ and His mother as your meditations on the Joyful, Luminous, Sorrowful, and Glorious mysteries reach a new level.

Contemplate the mystery of Christ.

Praying the Rosary is small enough to place on your nightstand, carry in your purse, or put in your pocket. Beautiful, four-color icons are shown for each mystery.

"To recite the Rosary is nothing other than to contemplate with Mary the face of Christ." — Pope John Paul II, *Rosarium Virginis Mariae*

Praying the Rosary
By Michael Dubruiel & Amy Welborn
1-59276-037-6 **(ID# T87)**, paper, 64 pp.

*Available at bookstores. Credit card customers can order direct from **Our Sunday Visitor** by calling **1-800-348-2440, ext. 3**. Order online at www.osv.com.*

OurSundayVisitor

200 Noll Plaza
Huntington, IN 46750

Periodicals • Books • Pamphlets • Tapes • Curricula • Software • Offering Envelopes
Website: www.osv.com • For a free catalog, call 1-800-348-2440
A49BBZBP

Our Sunday Visitor ...
Your Source for Discovering
the Riches of the Catholic Faith

Our Sunday Visitor has an extensive line of materials for young children, teens, and adults. Our books, Bibles, pamphlets, CD-ROMs, audios, and videos are available in bookstores worldwide.

To receive a FREE full-line catalog or for more information, call **Our Sunday Visitor** at **1-800-348-2440, ext. 3**. Or write **Our Sunday Visitor** / 200 Noll Plaza / Huntington, IN 46750.

Please send me ___ A catalog
Please send me materials on:
___ Apologetics and catechetics
___ Prayer books
___ The family
___ Reference works
___ Heritage and the saints
___ The parish

Name _____
Address _____ Apt._____
City _____ State _____ Zip_____
Telephone ( ) _____
                                                          A49BBBBP

Please send a friend ___ A catalog
Please send a friend materials on:
___ Apologetics and catechetics
___ Prayer books
___ The family
___ Reference works
___ Heritage and the saints
___ The parish

Name _____
Address _____ Apt._____
City _____ State _____ Zip_____
Telephone ( ) _____
                                                          A49BBBBP

OurSundayVisitor

200 Noll Plaza, Huntington, IN 46750
Toll free: **1-800-348-2440**
Website: www.osv.com